Teacher's Edition

BOOK

MW01283264

SRA
Open
Court
Reading

Lesson and Unit Assessment

Blackline Masters with Answer Key

Grade 2

McGraw Hill

mheducation.com/prek-12

Send all inquiries to:
McGraw Hill
8787 Orion Place
Columbus, OH 43240

ISBN: 978-1-26-560050-1
MHID: 1-26-560050-3

Printed in the United States of America.

5 6 7 8 9 10 11 12 13 LHN 28 27 26 25 24 23

C

Table of Contents

SRA Open Court Reading Assessment

SRA Open Court Reading focuses on helping students develop the abilities that are critical to reading with understanding. The assessments are designed to inform instruction while giving students an opportunity to practice and apply what they have learned.

The assessments that are featured in *SRA Open Court Reading* represent reasonable expectations for students at various grades. They reflect both the Common Core State Standards and the learning standards that have been adopted by various states. Research suggests that these skills are closely related to how well students learn to read a variety of texts with understanding.

SRA Open Court Reading has a four-step assessment cycle. It starts with a **Diagnostic Assessment** used for screening at the beginning of the year. Tools to monitor progress and differentiate instruction are built into each lesson. At the end of each lesson is a **Lesson Assessment**, and a **Unit Assessment** concludes each unit. A *Benchmark Assessment* is available to monitor student progress periodically over the course of the school year.

Diagnostic Assessment

A **Diagnostic Assessment** is included to help you identify student strengths, weaknesses, and areas of concern in the following six technical skill areas:

- Phonemic Awareness
- Phonics and Decoding
- Oral Reading Fluency
- Spelling
- Vocabulary
- Reading Comprehension

The Diagnostic Assessment can be used as an initial screener with individual students or groups of students who you observe might be lacking the prerequisite skills for the grade level. The information from the Diagnostic Assessment can then be used to inform instruction in those specific areas.

Students entering the classroom after the start of the year should be administered the Diagnostic Assessment to ascertain what grade-level material they know, in which skill areas they might need support, and whether they need immediate intervention. For example, students at this level who struggle with the Phonemic Awareness and Decoding assessments are much clearer candidates for some form of intervention than students who have difficulty with particular spelling constructions or unfamiliar vocabulary words.

As students complete the progress monitoring assessments, administer the Diagnostic Assessment to students whose performance deems them at risk for reading failure: students whose **Lesson and Unit Assessment** scores are below 70 percent, whose oral reading lacks key elements of prosody and is below the 50th percentile in words correct per minute (WCPM), and whose genre writing and extended response answers lack focus, organization, and clarity.

Students' results in the Diagnostic Assessment will assist you in making key instructional placement decisions. Use the results of these assessments to identify a student's reading needs. The Diagnostic Assessments contain material in the six technical skill areas in which an on-level student should be able to show proficiency, defined as a score of 80 percent or higher in the multiple-choice subtests and the appropriate WCPM for the time of the year. Students who score below the expected level on any of the technical skill areas will need to remedy this through additional scaffolding and support provided in the *Intervention Teacher's Guide* and *Intervention Support BLMs*.

You can use the Student Assessment Record to keep track of student performance in the Diagnostic Assessment. See page 214.

Lesson and Unit Assessments

Lesson Assessments cover the content of specific lessons, and **Unit Assessments** comprise all the content that was covered in the lessons within that unit. In most cases, content is tested at least twice within a unit, adding to the reliability of the assessment process.

The primary purpose of the Lesson Assessments is to allow the teacher to monitor student progress on a regular basis. This process makes it less likely that a student will fall behind because it gives teachers the opportunity to differentiate or repeat instruction as needed.

The Unit Assessments are summative in the sense that they represent a collection of related skills and are administered at the conclusion of a number of lessons. The goal of the unit assessment is to evaluate student proficiency of previously taught skills. The results serve as a summative assessment by providing a status of current achievement in relation to student progress through the curriculum. The results of the assessments can be used to inform subsequent instruction, aid in making leveling and grouping decisions, and point toward areas in need of reteaching or remediation.

Although the assessments are tied closely to the instructional path featured in **SRA Open Court Reading**, they may also be used independently because they reflect critical reading behaviors. For example, some assessments might be used to identify students who need the kind of supplemental instruction provided within *SRA Open Court Reading*. In kindergarten, the letter reading assessments lend themselves to this purpose, as do the fluency assessments in grades 1 through 3.

Assessment Item Types

Grade 2 assessments feature the following item types—selected response (SR), evidence-based selected response (EBSR), constructed response (CR), and technology-enhanced constructed response (TECR) items such as fill-in-the-blank, ordering, bucketing information, and circle or underline text. Each unit features a performance task (PT) assessment in a previously taught genre. (Note that the print versions of TECR items are available in this component; the full functionality of the items is available only through the online assessment.) This variety of item types provides multiple methods of assessing student understanding and allows for deeper investigation into skills and strategies. It also provides students an opportunity to become familiar with the kinds of questions they will encounter in state-mandated summative assessments.

Administering the Assessments

Almost all of the grade 2 assessments may be administered to the whole class. Students respond by filling in a bubble under the correct answer, constructing short written answers, and by crafting a longer, more detailed response to show comprehension of what they have read. The exception is the oral fluency assessment, which must be administered individually.

Lesson Assessments should be administered as closely as possible to the completion of the lesson. This proximity will make it more likely that the assessment will measure the student's acquisition of the skill. **Unit Assessments** should be administered close to the completion of a unit, but there is greater flexibility with the timing. The skills within a unit will have been practiced and measured several times before, making the Unit Assessment a reasonable measure of how well the skills have been retained.

Ideally, all students should complete all of the assessments. This level of fidelity will provide the teacher with a dependable measure of students' acquisition of the most important foundational skills. Comprehensive assessment will make it easier to identify students who are struggling, provide them with additional instruction and practice, and prevent them from falling further behind.

Review the assessments before administering them so you are familiar with the directions, which are on each page. Duplicate a copy of the corresponding student assessment blackline master for each student. Review the directions with students and tell them they will mark their answers on this page.

If the entire class is being assessed at the same time, testing can take place in the classroom. If only a small group of students or a single student is being assessed, a quiet corner of the classroom will work well. There should be relatively few distractions, and you should be able to sit beside or across from the student at a table or large desk. Follow the directions for administering the assessment. At the conclusion of the assessment, collect the assessments for scoring and record the results.

Organizing Assessment Results

The results of assessment are most useful when they are organized in a convenient and understandable way.

Observing students as they read anthology selections is an effective way to learn their strengths and areas of need in comprehension. Use the Comprehension Observation Log during class time to record your observations of students. See page 216. Choose a small set of students to focus on for a particular lesson. You might want to observe students more than once to get a clear idea of their comprehension of texts. Copy this page for each student or group of students you observe.

Make a copy of the Student Assessment Record for each student. See page 214. Enter the results of each lesson and unit assessment after they have been completed. On a regular basis, review student progress. This will provide an overview of the literacy status of a given student at any time in the school year.

Next, record the results on the Class Assessment Record. See pages 211–213. The chief purpose of this record is to help you identify students who have not yet demonstrated proficiency with specific skill clusters. These students can be grouped for additional instruction and practice in the skills as needed.

Make a copy of the Oral Fluency Assessment Record for each student. See page 215. Record the results of the oral fluency assessments after each lesson and unit assessment. When you record the results of the assessment, be sure to identify the cold and warm readings. The student's first attempt may be considered a "cold" reading, and the subsequent attempts are "warm" readings.

Additional Resources

Progress monitoring and instructional suggestions are provided on the following pages. However, additional information is provided online in the Resource Library. Refer to the *Assessment Handbook* and the *Intervention Teacher's Guide* for instructional suggestions to help students progress toward proficiency. The *Comprehension and Vocabulary Assessments* provide students with a new reading selection and help to develop the abilities critical to reading with understanding.

The purpose of the *Assessment Handbook* is to help you manage the use of multiple assessments, interpret the results, and use that information for instructional planning. It will provide you with basic definitions and clear guidance on how test scores can be a useful resource for addressing your students' needs.

The *Intervention Teacher's Guide* and *Intervention Support BLMs* provide 15–20 minutes of instructional materials daily to reinforce and extend the core **SRA Open Court Reading** lessons. The lessons will be used with small groups of struggling readers to pre-teach or reteach key elements of the core lesson.

The *Comprehension and Vocabulary Assessments* are designed to inform instruction while giving students an opportunity to practice and apply what they have learned. Use the weekly reading selections for comprehension and vocabulary assessment. The topic of the weekly reading selection connects to the lesson's essential question and genre focus. The comprehension assessment items align to the week's Access Complex Text Skill(s) and Writer's Craft elements. The vocabulary assessment items assess understanding and meaning of vocabulary words from the new reading selection.

Performance Expectations: Lesson Assessment

Each **Lesson Assessment** focuses on the following key areas:

- Phonics
- Vocabulary
- Comprehension
- Grammar, Usage, and Mechanics
- Oral Fluency

Lesson Assessments consist of the following:

Lesson Assessment	Format	Scope	Scoring
*Phonics	• Selected Response • Constructed Response	Sounds and Spellings	10 points (5 items x 2 points) **Acceptable Correct:** 4 out of 5 (items)
Vocabulary	• Selected Response	Selection Vocabulary	10 points (5 items x 2 points) **Acceptable Correct:** 8 out of 10 points

Comprehension	• Evidence-Based Selected Response
	• Selected Response
		Comprehension Skills	10 points
			1 item:
			    Part A = 1 point
			    Part B = 1 points
			4 items x 2 points
			Acceptable Correct:
			8 out of 10 points

	• Constructed Response	Comprehension Skills	10 points (5 items x 2 points) **Acceptable Correct:** 8 out of 10 points
	• Extended Response	Comprehension related to a selection	4 points Refer to p. xiii **Four Point Rubrics for Analyzing the Selection** **Goal Score:** 3 or higher
Grammar, Usage, and Mechanics	• Selected Response • Constructed Response	Grammar, Usage, and Mechanics skills practiced in the lesson	10 points (5 items x 2 points) **Acceptable Correct:** 8 out of 10 points
Oral Fluency	• Teacher-Directed • Student Performance	Oral fluency development from lesson to lesson	Refer to p. xi **Performance Expectations:** **Oral Fluency Assessment**

*The number of items may vary per Lesson Assessment.

Because the skills featured in **SRA Open Court Reading** are so critical to reading success, it is important that students demonstrate proficiency. Generally speaking, a score of 80% is acceptable.

Most of the Lesson Assessments in grade 2 consist of five selected response items (SR). For these assessments, **4 out of 5** items correct is acceptable. Ideally, students should eventually reach 100% correct at least occasionally.

The Comprehension assessment is a combination of selected response (SR) and constructed-response items (CR) that address the Access Complex Text and Writer's Craft skills taught that week. Each comprehension assessment begins with five selected response items. The first item is a two-part question. For this evidence-based selected response (EBSR) question, Part A is worth one point and Part B is worth one point. Students will need to compare their answer in Part A with the evidence-based answer choices in Part B. For these assessments, **8 out of 10** points is acceptable.

Next, students answer five questions that include a technology-enhanced constructed response (TECR) item and constructed response (CR) items. Each item is worth two points, for a total of ten points. For these assessments, **8 out of 10** points is acceptable.

For the constructed-response items, assign a score using the correct response parameters provided in the answer key along with the scoring rubrics shown below:

Constructed-Response Rubric

2 Points The response is well-crafted and concise and shows a thorough understanding of the underlying skill. Relevant evidence is used to answer the question.

1 Point The response shows partial understanding of the underlying skill. Evidence is included, but examples are too general.

0 Points Response shows a complete lack of understanding or is left blank.

The Analyzing the Selection assessment allows students to craft a longer, more detailed response to show comprehension of what they have read. It also provides additional data on students' writing skills as they progress through the program. These questions and prompts are worth four points each. A score of **3 or higher** is the goal score.

Use the following criteria to judge student responses. Explain the writing rubric at the start of the year and review again before implementing the assessment. See page xiii. This will help students understand the expectations that you have of their writing. To fully answer the question or prompt, student answers should be approximately eighty to one hundred and ten words.

Four Point Rubrics for Analyzing the Selection

Focus

4   The response answers the question thoroughly without wandering off topic.

3   The response answers the question partially and stays mostly on topic.

2   The response answers the question somewhat but wanders off topic.

1   The response fails to answer the question or does so minimally.

Ideas and Organization

4   The ideas are expressed clearly and meaningfully as they relate to the question.

3   Most of the ideas are related to the question and are expressed reasonably well.

2   Some of the ideas are meaningful, but they are not expressed clearly.

1   Few or no meaningful ideas are included in the response or they are expressed poorly.

Elaboration (Textual Support)

4   The response is thoroughly supported by references to the text.

3   The response is supported moderately by references to the text.

2   Some references to the text support the response.

1   Few or no references to the text are included in the response.

Conventions

4   There are few or no errors in writing conventions of the response.

3   The response has some errors, but they do not detract significantly from its meaning.

2   The number of errors in writing conventions makes reading the response difficult.

1   There are many errors in grammar, usage, spelling, and other conventions.

Performance Expectations: Unit Assessment

Each **Unit Assessment** focuses on the following key areas:

- Phonics
- Vocabulary
- Comprehension
- Grammar, Usage, and Mechanics
- Spelling
- Oral Fluency
- Writing

Unit Assessments consist of the following:

Unit Assessment	Format	Scope	Scoring
*****Phonics**	• Selected Response • Constructed Response	Sounds and Spellings practiced in the unit	2 points per item **Acceptable Correct:** Units 1 and 3: 40 out of 50 points Unit 2: 32 out of 40 points
Vocabulary	• Selected Response	Selection Vocabulary from the unit	30 points (10 items x 3 points) **Acceptable Correct:** 24 out of 30 points

Comprehension	• Evidence-Based Selected Response
	• Selected Response
		Comprehension Skills related to a new reading selection	10 points
			1 item:
			    Part A = 1 point
			    Part B = 1 point
			4 items x 1 point
			Acceptable Correct:
			8 out of 10 points

Grammar, Usage, and Mechanics	• Selected Response • Constructed Response	Grammar, Usage, and Mechanics skills practiced in the unit	20 points (10 items x 2 points) **Acceptable Correct:** 16 out of 20 points
Spelling	• Selected Response	Spelling words from the unit	10 points (10 items x 1 points) **Acceptable Correct:** 8 out of 10 points
Oral Fluency	• Teacher-Directed Student Performance	Oral fluency development from unit to unit	Refer to p. xi **Performance Expectations: Oral Fluency Assessment**
Writing	• Performance Task	Writing task based on a specific genre—Opinion, Informative, or Narrative	4 points Refer to pp. 84, 146, and 209 (Genre-specific four point writing rubrics) **Goal Score:** 3 points or higher

*The number of items may vary per Unit Assessment.

A score of 80% or higher on each Unit Assessment is expected. Students who consistently fall below 80% should be monitored for possible intervention. Additional scaffolding and support is provided in the *Intervention Teacher's Guide*.

The unit Vocabulary, Grammar, Usage and Mechanics, and Spelling assessments consist of ten items each. Students may respond by filling in a bubble under the correct answer and constructing short written answers for Grammar, Usage, and Mechanics assessments. For these assessments, **8 out of 10** items correct is acceptable.

The unit Comprehension assessments contain five selected response items, based on a new reading selection. The first item is a two-part question. For this evidence-based selected response (EBSR) question, Part A is worth one point and Part B is worth one point. Students will need to compare their answer in Part A with the evidence-based answer choices in Part B. For these assessments, **8 out of 10** points is acceptable.

At the end of each Unit Assessment, students will be given a writing task based on a specific genre—Opinion, Informative, or Narrative. These performance tasks reflect students' prior knowledge and experience with writing in a specific genre. Each writing assessment consists of the writing task; key reminders on how to best complete the writing task; and rubrics to judge student writing. Students will be graded on a 4-point scale. A score of **3 or higher** is the goal score.

Explain the writing rubrics at the start of the year and review again before implementing the writing tasks. See pages 84, 146, and 209. This will help students understand the expectations that you have of their writing. It also removes some of the mystery that students often associate with writing assignments.

Six Point Writing Rubrics for assessing student writing are also provided. See page 210. These can take the place of the four point rubrics if you are in a school that uses the six point rubric scoring system.

Monitoring Student Progress

It is important to keep in mind that not all students learn in the same way or at the same rate. Many factors affect student progress, especially in the early grades. They include early language exposure, socioeconomic status, and other factors. Moreover, individual students may acquire some skills at a different pace than other skills. Because of these sources of variance, we suggest several strategies.

- Evaluate progress over a reasonable time frame rather than at a single point.
- Do not hesitate to re-administer the same assessment several times when additional instruction and practice are provided. Research suggests that repeated assessment does not create a familiarity effect when feedback is not provided.
- When appropriate, allow students to move to new skills rather than limiting them to instruction and practice in only the skills with which they are struggling. For example, if students have not shown proficiency with digraph spellings, allow them to move on to other sound-spellings while continuing to practice digraphs.

One of the most beneficial practices associated with assessment is a review with the entire class. This should be undertaken only if you are sure that the assessments will not be administered again to any of the students. Once they receive feedback and clarification, the activity loses its value as an assessment.

The review should be considered a form of practice with feedback. Simply put, you repeat the assessment, including directions, and have students respond in a think-aloud format. When necessary, you can clarify the explanation associated with the correct answer and point out how the incorrect answers are wrong if you believe this will be helpful. The most important aspect of the review is emphasizing the correct answer using academic yet understandable language.

Speak clearly and use appropriate phrasing so that the students can understand you. If necessary, clarify words or constructs in the assessment prompts that may be unfamiliar to some students. Encourage students to contribute or ask questions. This type of interaction is extremely valuable to students because it presents them with an opportunity to process academic language in a way that is meaningful and not threatening. Moreover, it may help them approach future assessments not as situations to be feared but as opportunities to demonstrate what they know.

The primary data source provided by the assessments is the total score. This is the most dependable measure of a student's performance. If a student's performance is inconsistent or far below that of the other students in the group, you may choose to do an item analysis of the student's performance on selected assessments.

The item analysis procedure is straightforward. Choose the assessments in which you are interested and examine the student's performance at the item level. One approach is to skim the relevant assessments to see if a pattern of performance is evident. For example, does the student seem to choose correct answers to the easier items in a cluster? If so, the student might understand the underlying construct, like long *a* spellings, but might be unfamiliar with some of the words.

Another approach is to review a given assessment and have the student do an oral think-aloud item by item. This method is extremely informative because it gives insights into the cognitive processes that a student is using to choose an answer. Perhaps the greatest benefit is that it can confirm a student's understanding of the construct associated with the assessment.

Performance Expectations: Oral Fluency Assessment

Oral fluency assessment is a widely recognized method of evaluating how well students can read. In grade 2, oral fluency assessments take place at the end of every lesson and unit. The expectations for student performance are shown below. These expectations reflect what research suggests is acceptable performance for grade 2 students as represented by words correct per minute (WCPM).

Words Correct per Minute Expectations by Unit

Unit	1	2	3	4	5	6
WCPM	84	92	100	109	116	124

In addition to words correct per minute (WCPM), the Oral Fluency Assessment: Student Record includes a checklist for reading prosody. These are the qualitative characteristics of oral fluency like pace and intonation. The end-of-year expectation for students should be **four out of five prosody elements at the average level**.

Although the table above shows that student progress is consistently improving, this is rarely the case. The table reflects average scores that varied greatly among students. At the individual student level, there are many factors that can affect performance, including differences between passages, student learning rates, and conditions that might affect a student on a given day. Given these factors, it is likely that an individual student's performance will vary in a meaningful way both positively and negatively.

When to Administer

We encourage you to administer each oral fluency assessment more than once. The student's first attempt may be considered a "cold" reading, and the subsequent attempts are "warm" readings. You may even encourage the student to practice reading the fluency passage. When you record the results of the assessment in the Oral Fluency Assessment Record, be sure to identify the cold and warm readings. By the end of the school year, the student's scores for cold and warm oral fluency assessments should be approximately equal. The rationale for this expectation is that the student should be able to read new texts with a high degree of oral or silent fluency.

How to Administer

Have the student do a one-minute timed reading of a leveled passage and follow along on a copy of the same text, marking errors. Mistakes such as omissions, substitutions, insertions of words or parts of words, and hesitations of more than three seconds are errors; self-corrections and repetitions are not. Calculate the number of words read correctly per minute by subtracting the number of errors from the total number of words read.

Interpreting the Scores

Oral reading accuracy is a score based on the total number of words read and the number of errors noted. Those students below or significantly below the Words Correct per Minute Expectations by Unit are at possible risk of reading difficulties. Data gathered from the Oral Fluency Assessment Record may be used to verify or clarify instructional decisions.

If time permits, you may choose to do an analysis of the errors the student makes. Here are some examples.

- A student who reads highly decodable words well but has difficulty with less decodable words probably understands the most common sound-spellings. The student probably needs practice in reading common words that have uncommon sound-spellings.
- Inserting extra words suggests that the student comprehends the text but is reading impulsively. This student may benefit from paired reading with a competent reader.
- Note where errors occur in the text. If the errors increase toward the end of the passage, the student might be affected by fatigue. Conversely, if the errors are more frequent at the beginning of the text, the student might be using context to supplement decoding.

After the student's first attempt to read the text, you may choose to answer questions about the passage. Begin with literal questions that are relatively simple. As the student's ability improves, the questions can become more inferential. You may even ask the student to point to the text within the passage that supports the answer. A related task is to ask the student to retell the passage and include as many details as the student can recall. These activities will help you understand how well the student is reading with understanding.

Additional information is provided online in the Resource Library. Refer to the **Assessment Handbook** and the **Intervention Teacher's Guide** for instructional suggestions to help students progress towards proficiency.

Four Point Rubrics for Analyzing the Selection

Score	Focus	Ideas and Organization	Elaboration (Textual Support)	Conventions
4 Points	The response answers the question thoroughly without wandering off topic.	The ideas are expressed clearly and meaningfully as they relate to the question.	The response is thoroughly supported by references to the text.	There are few or no errors in writing conventions of the response.
3 Points	The response answers the question partially and stays mostly on topic.	Most of the ideas are related to the question and are expressed reasonably well.	The response is supported moderately by references to the text.	The response has some errors, but they do not detract significantly from its meaning.
2 Points	The response answers the question somewhat but wanders off topic.	Some of the ideas are meaningful, but they are not expressed clearly.	Some references to the text support the response.	The number of errors in writing conventions makes reading the response difficult.
1 Point	The response fails to answer the question or does so minimally.	Few or no meaningful ideas are included in the response or they are expressed poorly.	Few or no references to the text are included in the response.	There are many errors in grammar, usage, spelling, and other conventions.

Name _____ Date _____ Score _____

Diagnostic Assessment

Phonemic Awareness

Directions for Teacher: Make a copy of pages 1–4 for each student.

Teacher: Fill in the bubble for the sound that is at the *beginning* of tap . . . tap.

1. Ⓐ t   Ⓒ a
   Ⓑ p   Ⓓ e

Teacher: Fill in the bubble for the sound that is in the *middle* of sad . . . sad.

2. Ⓐ d   **Ⓒ a**
   Ⓑ s   Ⓓ t

Teacher: Fill in the bubble for the word with the long o sound. The words are *hop, hope, hat, hit.*

3. Ⓐ hop   Ⓒ hat
   Ⓑ hope   Ⓓ hit

Teacher: Fill in the bubble for the word with the short *a* sound. The words are *ship, shape, sat, sit.*

4. Ⓐ ship   **Ⓒ sat**
   Ⓑ shape   Ⓓ sit

Teacher: Which word belongs in this group of rhyming words? *glad, bad, mad*

5. Ⓐ bag   **Ⓒ sad**
   Ⓑ lag   Ⓓ doll

Diagnostic Assessment (continued)

Phonemic Awareness

Teacher: Which word does *not* belong in this group of rhyming words? *stand, land, and*

6. Ⓐ dance
   Ⓑ grand
   Ⓒ band
   Ⓓ hand

Teacher: Listen carefully. Start with *flight*. Drop the last sound. What new word do you have?

7. Ⓐ fight
   Ⓑ light
   Ⓒ fly
   Ⓓ tile

Teacher: Listen carefully. Start with *rhyme*. Change the /r/ to /t/. What new word do you have?

8. Ⓐ rye
   Ⓑ right
   Ⓒ tire
   Ⓓ time

Teacher: Listen carefully: /f/ /r/ /ē/. Fill in the bubble for the word /f/ /r/ /ē/.

9. Ⓐ fray
   Ⓑ fry
   Ⓒ free
   Ⓓ reef

Teacher: Listen carefully: /l/ /e/ /t/. Fill in the bubble for the word /l/ /e/ /t/.

10. Ⓐ lete
   Ⓑ let
   Ⓒ tell
   Ⓓ late

Diagnostic Assessment (continued)

Teacher: Fill in the bubble for the sound that is at the end of *tax . . . tax.*

11. Ⓐ a
    🅑 ks
    Ⓒ t
    Ⓓ s

Teacher: Fill in the bubble for the sound that is at the beginning of *chain . . . chain.*

12. Ⓐ a
    Ⓑ n
    🅒 ch
    Ⓓ c

Teacher: Fill in the bubble for the sound that is at the *beginning* of *mop . . . mop.*

13. 🅐 m
    Ⓑ p
    Ⓒ o
    Ⓓ e

Teacher: Fill in the bubble for the sound that is in the *middle* of *set . . . set.*

14. 🅐 e
    Ⓑ s
    Ⓒ a
    Ⓓ t

Teacher: Fill in the bubble for the word with the long *a* sound. The words are *map, make, deep, sit.*

15. Ⓐ map
    🅑 make
    Ⓒ deep
    Ⓓ sit

Diagnostic Assessment (continued)

Teacher: Fill in the bubble for the word with the short *u* sound. The words are *noon, fast, cup, hot.*

16. Ⓐ noon
Ⓑ fast
🅒 cup
Ⓓ hot

Teacher: Which word belongs in this group of rhyming words? *get, jet, met*

17. Ⓐ jam
Ⓑ stand
🅒 bet
Ⓓ deck

Teacher: Listen carefully: /s/ /u/ /n/. Fill in the bubble for the word /s/ /u/ /n/.

18. Ⓐ must
Ⓑ sent
🅒 sun
Ⓓ soon

Teacher: Fill in the bubble for the sound that is at the end of *head . . . head.*

19. Ⓐ e
🅑 d
Ⓒ t
Ⓓ a

Teacher: Which word belongs in this group of rhyming words? *part, start, dart*

20. Ⓐ shag
Ⓑ shark
🅒 cart
Ⓓ mark

Diagnostic Assessment (continued)

Phonics and Decoding

Directions for Teacher: Make a copy of pages 5–8 for each student.

Teacher: The word is *list*. Fill in the bubble for the word *list*.

1. (A) list
   (B) last
   (C) lies
   (D) lights

Teacher: Which spelling makes the sound /l/ . . . /l/?

2. (A) h
   (B) ll
   (C) ea
   (D) i

Teacher: Which word has the sound /j/ . . . /j/?

3. (A) gave
   (B) game
   (C) ginger
   (D) ring

Teacher: Fill in the bubble for the word *have . . . have*.

4. (A) huav
   (B) heave
   (C) have
   (D) haav

Teacher: Fill in the bubble for the word *said . . . said*.

5. (A) sad
   (B) sade
   (C) said
   (D) sawd

Diagnostic Assessment (continued)

Teacher: Which spelling makes the sound /or/?

6. Ⓐ **or**
Ⓑ ur
Ⓒ er
Ⓓ ar

Teacher: Which spelling makes the sound /er/?

7. Ⓐ or
Ⓑ **ur**
Ⓒ ere
Ⓓ ar

Teacher: The word is *jam*. Fill in the bubble for the word *jam*.

8. Ⓐ **jam**
Ⓑ gab
Ⓒ jar
Ⓓ mad

Teacher: Which spelling makes the sound /ē/ . . . /ē/?

9. Ⓐ or
Ⓑ **ea**
Ⓒ ll
Ⓓ sh

Teacher: Which word has the sound /ā/ . . . /ā/?

10. Ⓐ yes
Ⓑ lap
Ⓒ **gate**
Ⓓ won

Assessment 1

Diagnostic Assessment (continued)

Teacher: The word is *cool*. Fill in the bubble for the word *cool*.

11. **(A)** cool
    (B) coil
    (C) cook
    (D) coal

Teacher: The word is *bath*. Fill in the bubble for the word *bath*.

12. (A) bash
    (B) bat
    (C) bath
    (D) path

Teacher: Which spelling makes the sound /ā/ . . . /ā/?

13. **(A)** ai
    (B) ea
    (C) ch
    (D) el

Teacher: Which word has the sound /ī/ . . . /ī/?

14. **(A)** kite
    (B) cup
    (C) take
    (D) kit

Teacher: The word is *just*. Fill in the bubble for the word *just*.

15. (A) gust
    (B) just
    (C) gasp
    (D) jest

Diagnostic Assessment (continued)

Teacher: The word is *now*. Fill in the bubble for the word *now*.

16. Ⓐ mew
    Ⓑ mow
    Ⓒ new
    ⬤Ⓓ now

Teacher: Which word has the sound /v/ . . . /v/?

17. Ⓐ want
    Ⓑ fun
    ⬤Ⓒ vest
    Ⓓ yes

Teacher: Which spelling makes the sound /ē/ . . . /ē/?

18. Ⓐ or
    ⬤Ⓑ ee
    Ⓒ ll
    Ⓓ sh

Teacher: The word is *steep*. Fill in the bubble for the word *steep*.

19. Ⓐ step
    ⬤Ⓑ steep
    Ⓒ stop
    Ⓓ stem

Teacher: The word is *fire*. Fill in the bubble for the word *fire*.

20. ⬤Ⓐ fire
    Ⓑ fur
    Ⓒ fed
    Ⓓ file

Name _____ **Date** _____ **Score** _____

Diagnostic Assessment

Phonemic Awareness

1. Ⓐ t   Ⓒ a
    Ⓑ p   Ⓓ e

2. Ⓐ d   Ⓒ a
    Ⓑ s   Ⓓ t

3. Ⓐ hop   Ⓒ hat
    Ⓑ hope   Ⓓ hit

4. Ⓐ ship   Ⓒ sat
    Ⓑ shape   Ⓓ sit

5. Ⓐ bag   Ⓒ sad
    Ⓑ lag   Ⓓ doll

6. Ⓐ dance
   Ⓑ grand
   Ⓒ band
   Ⓓ hand

7. Ⓐ fight
   Ⓑ light
   Ⓒ fly
   Ⓓ tile

8. Ⓐ rye
   Ⓑ right
   Ⓒ tire
   Ⓓ time

9. Ⓐ fray
   Ⓑ fry
   Ⓒ free
   Ⓓ reef

10. Ⓐ lete
    Ⓑ let
    Ⓒ tell
    Ⓓ late

11. (A) a
(B) ks
(C) t
(D) s

12. (A) a
(B) n
(C) ch
(D) c

13. (A) m
(B) p
(C) o
(D) e

14. (A) e
(B) s
(C) a
(D) t

15. (A) map
(B) make
(C) deep
(D) sit

16. (A) noon
    (B) fast
    (C) cup
    (D) hot

17. (A) jam
    (B) stand
    (C) bet
    (D) deck

18. (A) must
    (B) sent
    (C) sun
    (D) soon

19. (A) e
    (B) d
    (C) t
    (D) a

20. (A) shag
    (B) shark
    (C) cart
    (D) mark

Diagnostic Assessment (continued)

Phonics and Decoding

1. Ⓐ list
Ⓑ last
Ⓒ lies
Ⓓ lights

2. Ⓐ h
Ⓑ ll
Ⓒ ea
Ⓓ i

3. Ⓐ gave
Ⓑ game
Ⓒ ginger
Ⓓ ring

4. Ⓐ huav
Ⓑ heave
Ⓒ have
Ⓓ haav

5. Ⓐ sad
Ⓑ sade
Ⓒ said
Ⓓ sawd

Diagnostic Assessment (continued)

6. (A) or
(B) ur
(C) er
(D) ar

7. (A) or
(B) ur
(C) ere
(D) ar

8. (A) jam
(B) gab
(C) jar
(D) mad

9. (A) or
(B) ea
(C) ll
(D) sh

10. (A) yes
(B) lap
(C) gate
(D) won

11. (A) cool
(B) coil
(C) cook
(D) coal

12. (A) bash
(B) bat
(C) bath
(D) path

13. (A) ai
(B) ea
(C) ch
(D) el

14. (A) kite
(B) cup
(C) take
(D) kit

15. (A) gust
(B) just
(C) gasp
(D) jest

16. Ⓐ mew
Ⓑ mow
Ⓒ new
Ⓓ now

17. Ⓐ want
Ⓑ fun
Ⓒ vest
Ⓓ yes

18. Ⓐ or
Ⓑ ee
Ⓒ ll
Ⓓ sh

19. Ⓐ step
Ⓑ steep
Ⓒ stop
Ⓓ stem

20. Ⓐ fire
Ⓑ fur
Ⓒ fed
Ⓓ file

Diagnostic • Oral Fluency Assessment: Student Record

Name _____ Date _____

Teacher Directions: Duplicate this page for each student you choose to assess. Make one copy of the Diagnostic Oral Fluency Assessment found on page 238 for students to read from.

Ann was going to see her grandmother, and she | 1-9
was bringing her a surprise. | 10-14

Mother said, "Do you think Grandmother will like | 15-22
her new friend?" | 23-25

"I think so," said Ann. "She likes cats." | 26-33

A little kitten was sitting in Ann's lap. The kitten | 34-43
was purring softly. | 44-46

"Will you be sad when you give Fluffy to | 47-55
Grandmother?" asked Mother. | 56-58

"No," said Ann. "We have our own cats, and I want | 59-69
Grandmother to have a friend." | 70-74

Ann's mother stopped the car. She got out of the | 75-84
car and opened the door for Ann. | 85-91

Ann got out of the car. She carried Fluffy in her | 92-102
arms. They walked to the porch, and Mother | 103-110
knocked on the door. Ann couldn't wait to see | 111-119
Grandmother's face. | 120-121

Evaluating Codes for Oral Fluency	
sky	(/) words read incorrectly
blue ^ sky	(^) Inserted word ([]) after the last word

Reading Rate and Accuracy	
Total Words Read	
Number of Errors	
Number of Correct Words Read per Minute (WCPM)	
Accuracy Rate	
(Number of Correct Words Read per Minute ÷ Total Words Read)	

Reading Prosody	LOW	AVG.	HIGH
Decoding Ability	○	○	○
Pace	○	○	○
Syntax	○	○	○
Self-correction	○	○	○
Intonation	○	○	○

Oral Fluency Passage Information	
Lexile Measure	380L
Mean Sentence Length	8.07
Mean Log Word Frequency	3.88
Word Count	121

Diagnostic Assessment (continued)

Spelling

Read each item. Fill in the bubble for the answer you think is correct.

1. The <u>lann</u> needs to be cut.
- Ⓐ lawan
- Ⓑ lauwn
- Ⓒ lawn
- Ⓓ Leave as is.

2. This <u>mousic</u> is great.
- Ⓐ music
- Ⓑ moosic
- Ⓒ mosic
- Ⓓ Leave as is.

3. This rock is <u>hird</u>.
- Ⓐ hard
- Ⓑ hoird
- Ⓒ heird
- Ⓓ Leave as is.

4. This soup is <u>good</u>.
- Ⓐ godd
- Ⓑ goud
- Ⓒ gode
- Ⓓ Leave as is.

5. Her dog is over <u>thair</u>.
- Ⓐ ther
- Ⓑ there
- Ⓒ thare
- Ⓓ Leave as is.

6. We <u>cowd</u> go to the zoo.
- Ⓐ cold
- Ⓑ cood
- Ⓒ could
- Ⓓ Leave as is.

7. The queen wore a <u>croun</u>.
- Ⓐ croon
- Ⓑ crown
- Ⓒ croan
- Ⓓ Leave as is.

8. The game ended <u>because</u> of rain.
- Ⓐ becuse
- Ⓑ becoose
- Ⓒ becoase
- Ⓓ Leave as is.

Read each item. Fill in the bubble for the answer you think is correct.

9. Ruth has a loud <u>voece</u>.
(A) voice
(B) voace
(C) veice
(D) Leave as is.

10. That truck is <u>houge</u>.
(A) hoge
(B) hige
(C) huge
(D) Leave as is.

11. The <u>coest</u> is pretty here.
(A) coast
(B) coist
(C) coust
(D) Leave as is.

12. Let's wait for a <u>waile</u>.
(A) woil
(B) weile
(C) while
(D) Leave as is.

13. Dad will <u>woush</u> the car.
(A) wash
(B) wush
(C) wosh
(D) Leave as is.

14. What is that <u>noese</u>?
(A) noase
(B) nouse
(C) noise
(D) Leave as is.

15. Who lives in this <u>hoose</u>?
(A) hoise
(B) house
(C) hoase
(D) Leave as is.

Diagnostic Assessment (continued)

Vocabulary

Read each item. Fill in the bubble for the answer you think is correct.

1. One person who wears a <u>uniform</u> is
   - Ⓐ a boy eating lunch.
   - Ⓑ a man driving to the store.
   - Ⓒ a firefighter going to a fire.
   - Ⓓ a girl jumping rope.

2. In which category, or group, would you put the word <u>meadow</u>?
   - Ⓐ animal
   - Ⓑ tree
   - Ⓒ field
   - Ⓓ fish

3. The kids are <u>forming</u> something outside. They are
   - Ⓐ making a snowperson.
   - Ⓑ walking on the sidewalk.
   - Ⓒ washing a car.
   - Ⓓ riding skateboards.

4. In which category, or group, would you put the word <u>riddles</u>?
   - Ⓐ reports
   - Ⓑ dances
   - Ⓒ experiments
   - Ⓓ puzzles

5. A woman <u>inspecting</u> a car would be
   - Ⓐ getting into it quickly.
   - Ⓑ looking at it closely.
   - Ⓒ driving it slowly.
   - Ⓓ washing it carefully.

Diagnostic Assessment (continued)

6. If you <u>recycled</u> a newspaper, you
(A) used it again.
(B) read a story.
(C) threw it out.
(D) went to school.

7. In which category, or group, would you put the word <u>dew</u>?
(A) water
(B) wind
(C) dirt
(D) clouds

8. Who is a person whose job is <u>protecting</u> others?
(A) ballerina
(B) police officer
(C) cashier
(D) banker

9. If you <u>stomped</u>, you
(A) jumped high.
(B) yelled loudly.
(C) ran fast.
(D) walked heavily.

10. In which category, or group, would you put the word <u>shrub</u>?
(A) fish
(B) rocks
(C) bushes
(D) books

11. Which are things that you would put in the category, or group, of school <u>supplies</u>?
(A) hammer and nails
(B) pencils and paper
(C) shovels
(D) dishes

12. If something is <u>rooted</u>, it is
(A) loose.
(B) a type of play.
(C) bumpy.
(D) fixed firmly.

13. The two words in <u>wetlands</u> tell you that they are
(A) highways.
(B) paths.
(C) hills.
(D) swamps.

14. Something that was NOT <u>invented</u> is
(A) a computer.
(B) a lawnmower.
(C) a tree.
(D) a telephone.

15. In which category, or group, would you put the word <u>insects</u>?
(A) fish
(B) plants
(C) bugs
(D) people

Diagnostic Assessment (continued)

Comprehension (Cold Read)

**Read the story. Then answer the questions. Fill in the
bubble for the answer you think is correct.**

A Surprise for Gran

The plane landed at the airport. The people got off the plane.
John saw his grandmother. He ran to her. Gran gave him a hug.

John and his dad picked up the bags. Mom waited with Gran.
Then they walked up steps to the parking lot.

In the car, John told Gran about his surprise. It had four legs,
a tail, and a wet nose.

1. How does John feel when he sees his grandmother?
- Ⓐ happy
- Ⓑ surprised
- Ⓒ sad
- Ⓓ mad

2. What is the main idea of the story?
- Ⓐ John goes to visit Gran.
- Ⓑ Gran visits John's family.
- Ⓒ Gran gets a new car.
- Ⓓ John flies on a plane.

3. What do John and his family do last?

Ⓐ go to the car

Ⓑ meet Gran

Ⓒ get the bags

Ⓓ hug Gran

4. How does everyone get to the parking lot?

Ⓐ by car

Ⓑ by elevator

Ⓒ by walking

Ⓓ by taxi

5. The surprise is

Ⓐ a puppy.

Ⓑ some flowers.

Ⓒ a new house.

Ⓓ a new bike.

Read the story. Then answer the questions. Fill in the bubble for the answer you think is correct.

The Yard Sale

Mom wanted to have a yard sale. "We have too many things," she said. "It's time to get rid of some things."

Dad, Liz, and Penny got to work. They cleaned out the garage. Liz put all her old toys in a box. Penny picked out the clothes that were too small. Mom set up tables in the yard. They put all the things out to sell.

"No one will buy this junk!" Penny said.

People came to the yard sale all day. Finally, it was over. "We worked hard, and I am hungry," Mom said. She shook the money box. It was full. "Now we can buy a nice dinner," she said.

6. Why do people have yard sales?
   Ⓐ to buy a new table
   Ⓑ to get rid of things
   Ⓒ to buy dinner
   Ⓓ to keep their things

7. Who puts clothes in the yard sale?
- Ⓐ Liz
- Ⓑ Mom
- Ⓒ Penny
- Ⓓ Dad

8. Why does Penny think no one will buy their stuff?
- Ⓐ She thinks it is new.
- Ⓑ She thinks it is broken.
- Ⓒ She thinks it is junk.
- Ⓓ She thinks it is nice.

9. How do you know the family sells many things?
- Ⓐ The box is filled with money.
- Ⓑ They clean out the garage.
- Ⓒ Liz sells her old toys.
- Ⓓ They are hungry.

10. What will the family do with the money?
- Ⓐ They will buy new clothes.
- Ⓑ They will take a trip.
- Ⓒ They will go out to dinner.
- Ⓓ They will fix the garage.

Read the story. Then answer the questions. Fill in the bubble for the answer you think is correct.

Jack's Shoe

It was time for Jack to go to school. He could not find his shoe. Jack looked all over the house. The shoe was nowhere. Jack's dog, Piper, came to Jack. Piper barked and went to the backyard. Jack followed him. Piper went into his doghouse. Jack looked inside. He was surprised. There was his shoe! "Now I know who took my shoe," Jack said.

11. Who is the main character of the story?
- Ⓐ Piper
- Ⓑ Jack
- Ⓒ Dad
- Ⓓ Mom

12. Where does most of the story take place?
- Ⓐ Jack's backyard
- Ⓑ Jack's school
- Ⓒ a baseball game
- Ⓓ the store

Diagnostic Assessment (continued)

13. What is the plot, or main idea, of the story?
    - Ⓐ Jack lives in the doghouse.
    - Ⓑ Jack goes to school.
    - Ⓒ Jack loses his shoe.
    - Ⓓ Piper eats Jack's shoe.

14. What happens in the middle of the story?
    - Ⓐ Jack goes to the backyard.
    - Ⓑ Jack goes to school.
    - Ⓒ Piper steals Jack's shoe.
    - Ⓓ Jack finds his shoe.

15. What happens at the end of the story?
    - Ⓐ Jack finds the shoe under the bed.
    - Ⓑ Jack is late for school.
    - Ⓒ Jack finds the shoe in the doghouse.
    - Ⓓ Jack looks for the shoe in the house.

Diagnostic Assessment (continued)

Read the story. Then answer the questions. Fill in the bubble for the answer you think is correct.

A Spring Surprise

Anna lived on a farm. Every day she collected eggs from the chickens. One spring day she went to the chicken house. There were no eggs. Then she heard a sound. She turned around. A chicken walked by. Ten yellow chicks ran behind her. Anna smiled. "That's what happened to the eggs!" she said.

16. Who is the main character of the story?
- (A) a chicken
- (B) Anna
- (C) Mom
- (D) Dad

17. Where does most of the story take place?
- (A) Anna's farm
- (B) school
- (C) the city
- (D) Anna's house

18. What is the plot, or main idea, of the story?
- Ⓐ Anna goes to school.
- Ⓑ There are many eggs.
- Ⓒ The eggs are missing.
- Ⓓ Anna lives on a farm.

19. What happens in the beginning of the story?
- Ⓐ Anna cannot find the eggs.
- Ⓑ Chicks chase Anna.
- Ⓒ The chickens hide the eggs.
- Ⓓ Anna finds the eggs.

20. What happens at the end of the story?
- Ⓐ Anna collects eggs.
- Ⓑ Anna hears a sound.
- Ⓒ Anna knows what happens to the eggs.
- Ⓓ A chicken walks by.

Phonics: /ch/ spelled *ch*, /th/ spelled *th*, /sh/ spelled *sh*, /w/ spelled *wh_*, /ar/ spelled *ar*

Fill in the bubble under the correct spelling of each word.

1. eath   each   eash
   ○   ○   ○

2. with   wich   wiph
   ○   ○   ○

3. thip   ship   stip
   ○   ○   ○

4. what   wat   wahat
   ○   ○   ○

5. fram   ferm   farm
   ○   ○   ○

The Mice Who Lived in a Shoe
Vocabulary

Read each item. Fill in the correct answer.

1. What does the word *timber* most likely mean in this sentence?
The ski lodge was made of *timber.*
- Ⓐ steel
- Ⓑ wood
- Ⓒ concrete
- Ⓓ sand

2. What does the word *fetched* mean in this sentence?
She *fetched* wood in the forest for the campfire.
- Ⓐ to feel respect for
- Ⓑ to put together in a pile
- Ⓒ went after and brought back
- Ⓓ threw away

3. What is a synonym for *merchant* in this sentence?
The *merchant* opened a general store in the small town.
- Ⓐ safety
- Ⓒ shelter
- Ⓑ builder
- Ⓓ buyer

4. What does the word *observed* mean in this sentence?
The scientists *observed* a comet in the night sky.
- Ⓐ looked at
- Ⓑ lifted up
- Ⓒ wrote about
- Ⓓ brought back

5. What does the word *platform* mean in this sentence?
We built a *platform* for the school play.
- Ⓐ a person who is good at sports
- Ⓑ a raised flat surface
- Ⓒ to come together
- Ⓓ to speak unclearly

The Mice Who Lived in a Shoe (continued)
Comprehension

Read the following items and fill in the correct answer.
You may look at the selection to answer the questions

1. The following question has two parts. First, answer **Part A.**
    Then, answer **Part B.**

    Part A In the beginning of the story, what is the biggest
    problem that the mouse family faces?
    Ⓐ feeling cold   Ⓑ getting wet   Ⓒ the cat   Ⓓ the wind

    Part B Which sentence from the story **best** supports your
    answer for **Part A**?
    Ⓐ When the wind blew, they flew all over the place.
    Ⓑ But the worst thing of all was when the cat put his paw
      into the shoe and stretched out his claws.
    Ⓒ The family huddled together at the toe end for safety.
    Ⓓ Pa looked at them carefully to see who had the best ideas.

2. What will the mice do to stay safe from the cat and the
    weather?
    Ⓐ The mice will move to a new shoe.
    Ⓑ The mice will become friends with the cat.
    Ⓒ The mice will chase the cat away.
    Ⓓ The mice will build a new house.

3. How do you know the shoe in the story is outside?
    Ⓐ It is in the rain, snow, and sun.
    Ⓑ The cat lives outside, too.
    Ⓒ The mice are able to run from the cat.
    Ⓓ It is where the mice live.

4. Which mouse in the story drew the dream house?
    Ⓐ Grandpa   Ⓑ Ma   Ⓒ Pa   Ⓓ Grandma

Comprehension

5. What was the effect of the merchant's visit?

Ⓐ The merchant had more money.

Ⓑ The mice had money for tools and materials.

Ⓒ The cat could not get the merchant.

Ⓓ The mice were able to buy a new house that was bigger.

Read the following items carefully. Answer the questions.

6. What are two materials that the mice use for their house?

_____

_____

7. What was the effect of Uncle Jack and Aunt Jane hearing that the mice were building a house?

_____

_____

8. What caused Sue and Pip to serve tea?

_____

_____

9. What are two examples from the story of characters working together?

_____

_____

10. Describe how Pa responds to challenges in the story.

_____

_____

The Mice Who Lived in a Shoe (continued)
Grammar, Usage, and Mechanics
Read each item. Fill in the correct answer.

1. Which of the words below is a common noun that is a place?
   - Ⓐ everyone
   - Ⓑ best
   - Ⓒ valley
   - Ⓓ string

2. Which of the words below is a common noun that is a person?
   - Ⓐ friend
   - Ⓑ window
   - Ⓒ broken
   - Ⓓ served

3. Which of the words below is a common noun that is a thing?
   - Ⓐ overjoyed
   - Ⓑ lovely
   - Ⓒ uncle
   - Ⓓ furniture

4. Which of the words below is a proper noun?
   - Ⓐ curtains
   - Ⓑ Grandma
   - Ⓒ enough
   - Ⓓ helped

5. Which of the words below is a proper noun that is a place?
   - Ⓐ Balcony
   - Ⓑ Mick
   - Ⓒ Chicago
   - Ⓓ House

Name _____ Date _____ Score _____

The Mice Who Lived in a Shoe (continued)
Analyzing the Selection

Read the question below. Write complete sentences for your answer. Support your answer with evidence from the selection.

How do you know that the mouse family is happy with their new home?

_____

_____

_____

_____

_____

_____

_____

_____

_____

_____

_____

_____

_____

_____

_____

_____

Teacher Directions: Duplicate this page for each student you choose to assess. Make one copy of the Unit 1 Lesson 1 Oral Fluency Assessment found on page 217 for students to read from.

Mice like to live near people. There is a reason for this. People live in houses, and they cook and eat in their houses. This is perfect for mice because it means they have places to live. They also have food to eat. | 1-10
11-19
20-29
30-38
39-43

There are many different kinds of mice. Some live near people, but others live in the wild. They don't like living near people. They know how to find food and make a home without people. | 44-51
52-61
62-70
71-78

In the wild, mice eat different kinds of food. They like seeds and nuts. They are very smart, and they are also very careful. That is because other animals like to eat mice. | 79-88
89-98
99-107
108-111

Evaluating Codes for Oral Fluency

sky	(/) words read incorrectly
blue ^ sky	(^) Inserted word ([]) after the last word

Reading Rate and Accuracy

Total Words Read	
Number of Errors	
Number of Correct Words Read per Minute (WCPM)	
Accuracy Rate	
(Number of Correct Words Read per Minute ÷ Total Words Read)	

Reading Prosody

	LOW	AVG.	HIGH
Decoding Ability	○	○	○
Pace	○	○	○
Syntax	○	○	○
Self-correction	○	○	○
Intonation	○	○	○

Oral Fluency Passage Information

Lexile Measure	450L
Mean Sentence Length	8.54
Mean Log Word Frequency	3.81
Word Count	111

Phonics: Closed Syllables

Look at each word. Think about how the words are divided into syllables. Fill in the bubble under the answer that shows if the word has *closed* or *not closed* syllables.

1. farmer

Closed   Not Closed

○   ○

2. above

Closed   Not Closed

○   ○

3. pencil

Closed   Not Closed

○   ○

4. money

Closed   Not Closed

○   ○

5. behind

Closed   Not Closed

○   ○

Phonics: /j/ spelled ■dge, /k/ spelled ■ck, /ch/ spelled ■tch

Fill in the bubble under the correct spelling of each word.

6. edje   eije   edge
   ○   ○   ○

7. bast   back   bacck
   ○   ○   ○

8. cadch   catsh   catch
   ○   ○   ○

9. bridge   brige   bridje
   ○   ○   ○

10. roch   rock   rokk
   ○   ○   ○

Ants and Aphids Work Together
Vocabulary

Read each item. Fill in the correct answer.

1. What is a synonym for *relationship* in this sentence?
The *relationship* between people and nature is important.
- (A) disguise
- (B) twisting
- (C) neighborhood
- (D) connection

2. What does the word *predators* mean in this sentence?
Hawks are *predators* for small mammals, like mice.
- (A) animals that are hunters
- (B) young ducks
- (C) people who work together
- (D) people who do an activity

3. What does the word *colony* most likely mean in this sentence?
There is a prairie dog *colony* in the park.
- (A) fur
- (B) group
- (C) symbiosis
- (D) growl

4. What is a synonym for *scurry* in this sentence?
The crabs tried to *scurry* away when they saw us.
- (A) sorry
- (B) roll
- (C) hurry
- (D) dig

5. What does the word *shelter* mean in this sentence?
We stayed under the *shelter* when the storm came.
- (A) ranch
- (B) safe place
- (C) long boat
- (D) liquid

Ants and Aphids Work Together (continued)
Comprehension

Read the following items carefully and fill in the correct answer. You may look back at the selection to answer the questions.

1. The following question has two parts. First, answer **Part A.** Then, answer **Part B.**

   Part A Which answer **best** describes ants and aphids?
   (A) Ants like to eat aphids.
   (B) Aphids like to eat ants.
   (C) They are both afraid of ladybugs.
   (D) They work together.

   Part B Which sentence from the story **best** supports your answer for **Part A**?
   (A) Aphids sometimes suck all the juices from a plant.
   (B) A hungry ant waits nearby.
   (C) In a busy forest, ants and aphids are a team.
   (D) Ants sometimes even eat ladybug eggs.

2. Ants rub aphids to get honeydew. This is most like
   (A) friends playing sports.
   (B) fathers driving a car.
   (C) mothers dressing children.
   (D) farmers milking cows.

3. Aphids are different from ants because
   (A) ants don't live in the forest.
   (B) ants don't produce honeydew.
   (C) aphids are much bigger than ants.
   (D) aphids bite ladybugs and other predators.

Ants and Aphids Work Together (continued)
Comprehension

4. The main idea of this story is that
   - Ⓐ ladybugs attack ants and aphids.
   - Ⓑ ants and aphids help one another.
   - Ⓒ honeydew must taste good to ants.
   - Ⓓ only ants live in colonies.

5. Why did the author write this story?
   - Ⓐ To show the reader where to find aphids.
   - Ⓑ To tell a funny story that readers would enjoy.
   - Ⓒ To inform readers about ants and aphids.
   - Ⓓ To persuade readers that ants are smart.

Read the following items carefully. Answer the questions.

6. How do the headings help contribute to the author's purpose?

   _____

7. What is a big difference between ants and ladybugs when it comes to aphids?

   _____

8. Why do ants carry aphids to new plants?

   _____

9. Ant colonies are usually underground. How does this help to keep aphid eggs safe?

   _____

10. Draw a line under the word in the sentence below that helps you know that honeydew is a liquid.

    Ants drink the honeydew that comes out.

Comprehension • *Assessment 1*

Ants and Aphids Work Together (continued)

Grammar, Usage, and Mechanics

Read each item. Fill in the correct answer.

1. Which of the words below is an action verb?
- Ⓐ swim
- Ⓑ water
- Ⓒ wet
- Ⓓ deep

2. Which of the words below is an action verb, not a helping verb or linking verb?
- Ⓐ have
- Ⓑ will
- Ⓒ find
- Ⓓ was

3. In which sentence is there an action verb?
- Ⓐ No, the aphid is safe.
- Ⓑ Ladybugs are predators.
- Ⓒ Was the aphid in danger?
- Ⓓ Aphids suck juices from plants.

4. In which sentence is there an action verb?
- Ⓐ The drop of water was big.
- Ⓑ Leaves fell from the tree.
- Ⓒ When is the school play?
- Ⓓ This was my grandmother's watch.

5. Which word in this sentence is an action verb?
Some animals hunt at night.
- Ⓐ some
- Ⓑ animals
- Ⓒ hunt
- Ⓓ night

Ants and Aphids Work Together (continued)
Analyzing the Selection

Read the question below. Write complete sentences for your answer. Support your answer with evidence from the selection.

What is the most important thing that ants do for aphids?

_____

_____

_____

_____

_____

_____

_____

_____

_____

_____

_____

_____

_____

_____

_____

_____

_____

_____

_____

Teacher Directions: Duplicate this page for each student you choose to assess. Make one copy of the Unit 1 Lesson 2 Oral Fluency Assessment found on page 218 for students to read from.

Many animals live in colonies. These are groups of animals. Ants live in colonies. They dig tunnels under the ground. The tunnels go far into the ground. They have spaces for ants to sleep. There are spaces for food. There are even spaces for ant eggs and babies.	1-8 9-17 18-26 27-35 36-45 46-48
Prairie dogs also live in colonies. These are animals that live on the western plains. They dig holes in the ground. A prairie dog colony can have ten or more families.	49-56 57-65 66-75 76-79
The holes that prairie dogs make are very important. They help the animals stay warm in winter and cool in summer. They also keep rain from flooding the colony. Prairie dogs are smart, but they are also cute. People love to watch them poke their heads out of their holes.	80-87 88-95 96-104 105-112 113-122 123-129

Evaluating Codes for Oral Fluency

sky	(/) words read incorrectly
blue ^ sky	(^) Inserted word ([ ]) after the last word

Reading Rate and Accuracy

Total Words Read	
Number of Errors	
Number of Correct Words Read per Minute (WCPM)	
Accuracy Rate	
(Number of Correct Words Read per Minute ÷ Total Words Read)	

Reading Prosody

	LOW	AVG.	HIGH
Decoding Ability	○	○	○
Pace	○	○	○
Syntax	○	○	○
Self-correction	○	○	○
Intonation	○	○	○

Oral Fluency Passage Information

Lexile Measure	480L
Mean Sentence Length	7.59
Mean Log Word Frequency	3.51
Word Count	129

Phonics: /ch/ spelled *ch*, /th/ spelled *th*, /sh/ spelled *sh*, /w/ spelled *wh_*, /ar/ spelled *ar*

Fill in the bubble under the correct spelling of each word.

1. wehn   when   hwen
    ○   ○   ○

2. shair   scair   chair
    ○   ○   ○

3. hard   hird   hord
    ○   ○   ○

4. chank   thank   trank
    ○   ○   ○

5. wash   wach   watsh
    ○   ○   ○

Phonics: /j/ spelled ■dge, /k/ spelled ■ck, /ch/ ■tch

Fill in the bubble under the correct spelling of each word.

6. duck   duch   dukk

   ○   ○   ○

7. juje   judge   jujge

   ○   ○   ○

8. kick   kikk   kict

   ○   ○   ○

9. watsh   wacth   watch

   ○   ○   ○

10. bagje   badge   batje

   ○   ○   ○

Phonics: Inflectional Endings –ed, –s, –es, and Closed Syllables

Fill in the bubble under the correct spelling of each word.

11. jumpded   jumpt   jumped
     ○   ○   ○

12. bells   bellz   belles
     ○   ○   ○

13. boxs   boxes   boxez
     ○   ○   ○

Look at the words in each group. Think about how the words are divided into syllables. Fill in the bubble under the word in each group that has *closed* syllables.

14. able   music   turkey
     ○   ○   ○

15. window   belong   open
     ○   ○   ○

The Bat, Birds, and Beasts
Vocabulary

Read each item. Fill in the correct answer.

1. What does the word *annual* mean in this sentence?
   The class picnic is an *annual* event.
   - Ⓐ in the afternoon
   - Ⓑ at school
   - Ⓒ every year
   - Ⓓ in a park

2. What is a synonym for *strategy* in this sentence?
   The team's *strategy* was to play slowly.
   - Ⓐ plan
   - Ⓑ work
   - Ⓒ jump
   - Ⓓ ball

3. What does the word *accepted* most likely mean in this sentence?
   The boss *accepted* the worker's idea.
   - Ⓐ made fun of
   - Ⓑ said yes to
   - Ⓒ told other people
   - Ⓓ wrote on paper

4. What does the word *emphasize* mean in this sentence?
   We *emphasize* that you be gentle with the kittens.
   - Ⓐ to allow
   - Ⓑ to pretend
   - Ⓒ to forgive
   - Ⓓ give special importance

5. What is a synonym for *inquired* in this sentence?
   My friend *inquired* about my new puppy.
   - Ⓐ dressed
   - Ⓑ hopped
   - Ⓒ painted
   - Ⓓ asked

The Bat, Birds, and Beasts (continued)
Comprehension

Read the following items carefully and fill in the correct answer. You may look back at the selection to answer the questions.

1. The following question has two parts. First, answer **Part A.** Then, answer **Part B.**

   Part A Which sentence from the story shows that Bat was very competitive?
   Ⓐ Who would win?
   Ⓑ Bat entered the game.
   Ⓒ But which team should he choose?
   Ⓓ He got very angry if he lost.

   Part B Which of these actions shows how competitive Bat really was?
   Ⓐ He said he had fur, claws, and teeth.
   Ⓑ He switched teams so he could win.
   Ⓒ He asked where he belonged.
   Ⓓ He spread his wings out to look like a bird.

2. What made Bat like the Birds?
   Ⓐ He had a beak.   Ⓒ He had wings.
   Ⓑ He had feathers.   Ⓓ He had an advantage.

3. Bat was different from the other Beasts because he
   Ⓐ was smaller than the others.
   Ⓑ wore the team jersey.
   Ⓒ had more teeth than the others.
   Ⓓ was loyal to the Birds.

The Bat, Birds, and Beasts (continued)
Comprehension

4. What is the author trying to describe with this sentence?
Stealthily, he crept over to the Beasts' side.
Ⓐ The Beasts were going to win the game.
Ⓑ Bat snuck over so no one would notice.
Ⓒ Vulture thought Bat looked like a piece of meat.
Ⓓ Hummingbird got mad when he recognized Bat.

5. How do you know the story is a fable?
Ⓐ The setting is in a big city.
Ⓑ The animals act like people.
Ⓒ Bat was able to fly.
Ⓓ The animals had fur and teeth.

Read the following items carefully. Answer the questions.

6. How were the Birds and Beasts different in the story?

_____

7. What does it mean when the story says that Bat would have more game time with the Birds?

_____

8. What does the phrase "hardly visible" mean in this sentence? Bat folded his wings back so they were hardly visible.

_____

9. Do you think Bat should be categorized as a Bird or Beast?

_____

10. A fable usually has a lesson. What lesson do you think Bat learned?

_____

Name _____ **Date** _____ **Score** _____

The Bat, Birds, and Beasts (continued)
Grammar, Usage, and Mechanics
Read each item. Fill in the correct answer.

1. Which helping verb fits best in this sentence?

The wind _____ blowing very hard.

Ⓐ has   Ⓒ is

Ⓑ can   Ⓓ are

2. Which linking verb fits best in this sentence?

Her friends _____ not here.

Ⓐ are   Ⓒ is

Ⓑ was   Ⓓ am

3. Which linking verb fits best in this sentence?

Some bats _____ in the cave.

Ⓐ was   Ⓒ is

Ⓑ were   Ⓓ am

4. Which helping verb fits best in this sentence?

The dog _____ chewing a really big bone.

Ⓐ had   Ⓒ did

Ⓑ can   Ⓓ was

5. Which linking verb fits best in this sentence?

My cousin _____ here last week.

Ⓐ came   Ⓒ are

Ⓑ was   Ⓓ visited

The Bat, Birds, and Beasts (continued)
Analyzing the Selection

Read the question below. Write complete sentences for your answer. Support your answer with evidence from the selection.

At the end of the story, neither the Beasts nor the Birds wanted Bat on their team. Why did they not want him?

_____

_____

_____

_____

_____

_____

_____

_____

_____

_____

_____

_____

_____

_____

_____

_____

_____

_____

_____

Teacher Directions: Duplicate this page for each student you choose to assess. Make one copy of the Unit 1 Lesson 3 Oral Fluency Assessment found on page 219 for students to read from.

Many animals work together. A good example is bees. When a bee finds a good flower, it goes back to the hive. The bee does a special dance. The way it dances tells the other bees where the flowers are.	1-8 9-19 20-30 31-40
The name of the place where a bee lives is a hive. A bee hive shows how good bees are at working together. They all help to build the hive. It would be impossible for one bee to make a hive.	41-51 52-61 62-71 72-81
Bees make their hives in holes in the ground or in trees. Sometimes people help them. They make special boxes. The bees make a hive in the box.	82-91 92-99 100-109
The inside of a bee hive is amazing. It is made up of little wax boxes with six sides called cells. The cells form a honey comb. The bees make the cells of wax. The inside of each cell is filled with honey.	110-121 122-131 132-141 142-152

Evaluating Codes for Oral Fluency

sky	(/) words read incorrectly
blue ^ sky	(^) Inserted word ([ ]) after the last word

Reading Rate and Accuracy

Total Words Read	
Number of Errors	
Number of Correct Words Read per Minute (WCPM)	
Accuracy Rate	
(Number of Correct Words Read per Minute ÷ Total Words Read)	

Reading Prosody

	LOW	AVG.	HIGH
Decoding Ability	○	○	○
Pace	○	○	○
Syntax	○	○	○
Self-correction	○	○	○
Intonation	○	○	○

Oral Fluency Passage Information

Lexile Measure	510L
Mean Sentence Length	8.44
Mean Log Word Frequency	3.63
Word Count	152

Phonics: /ng/ spelled *ng*, /nk/ spelled *nk*, and Inflectional Ending *-ing*

Fill in the bubble under the correct spelling of each word.

1. ragn   rang   raind
    ○   ○   ○

2. think   thinck   thingk
    ○   ○   ○

3. askng   asking   askeng
    ○   ○   ○

4. banck   banch   bank
    ○   ○   ○

5. sonk   sonp   song
    ○   ○   ○

Phonics: Schwa and /əl/ spelled *el*, *le*, *al*, *il*

Fill in the bubble under the correct spelling of each word.

6. seven   sevin   sevan
   ○   ○   ○

7. hullo   hallo   hello
   ○   ○   ○

8. appll   apple   appul
   ○   ○   ○

9. ulone   elone   alone
   ○   ○   ○

10. famly   family   famaly
   ○   ○   ○

A Cherokee Stickball Game
Vocabulary
Read each item. Fill in the correct answer.

1. What is a synonym for *furious* in this sentence? People were *furious* about the trash in the lake.
(A) frightened
(B) angry
(C) lucky
(D) bounced

2. What does the word *pity* mean in this sentence? It is a *pity* that it will rain on your birthday.
(A) a loud noise
(B) a reminder
(C) a feeling of sorrow
(D) a message

3. What does the word *humbly* most likely mean in this sentence? The people *humbly* greeted the king.
(A) without importance
(B) a little disappointed
(C) with lots of food
(D) wearing nice clothes

4. What does the word *part* mean in this sentence? This *part* of the garden is for corn.
(A) mile
(B) piece
(C) seed
(D) clear

5. What is a synonym for *roared* in this sentence? The crowd *roared* when the coach made a joke.
(A) smiled
(B) blocked
(C) named
(D) laughed

A Cherokee Stickball Game (continued)

Comprehension

Read the following items carefully and fill in the correct answer. You may look back at the selection to answer the questions.

1. The following question has two parts. First, answer **Part A.** Then, answer **Part B.**

   Part A Which answer **best** describes Big Bear?
   - Ⓐ He was happy to see Little Mouse.
   - Ⓑ He isn't interested in the game.
   - Ⓒ He doesn't seem very nice.
   - Ⓓ He likes to play stickball.

   Part B Which sentence from the story **best** supports your answer for **Part A**?
   - Ⓐ Little Mouse scurried to the Animal camp.
   - Ⓑ "What could *you* ever do for *us*?" Big Bear asked.
   - Ⓒ Both teams gathered at the field.
   - Ⓓ Big Bear roared with laughter.

2. How do you know the story is a folktale?
   - Ⓐ a bear is in the story
   - Ⓑ the mouse is small
   - Ⓒ there are drumbeats in the story
   - Ⓓ the animals are talking

3. How does Little Mouse change in the story?
   - Ⓐ He is given wings.
   - Ⓑ He becomes bigger.
   - Ⓒ He learns to play a drum.
   - Ⓓ He wants to play the game.

Comprehension • *Assessment 1*

A Cherokee Stickball Game (continued)
Comprehension

4. What did Little Mouse always want to be?
    Ⓐ a bat   Ⓑ a hero   Ⓒ a bird   Ⓓ a bear

5. Which sentence shows the lesson of the story?
    Ⓐ That meant the Birds were preparing for the big game!
    Ⓑ Pretty Feathered Eagle was circling high above the camp watching each of his players.
    Ⓒ In contrast, the Birds and Flying Bat came together as a team and won.
    Ⓓ He flew between the goal posts with the ball.

Read the following items carefully. Answer the questions.

6. Write two words from the story that match each character.
Big Bear   Little Mouse

_____   _____

_____   _____

7. What does it mean to say that Pretty Feathered Eagle had *a twinkle in his eye*?

_____

8. In your own words, tell how Little Mouse got his wings.

_____

_____

9. Why do you think the animals lost the game?

_____

10. How did Little Mouse know that the Birds were getting ready for the game?

_____

A Cherokee Stickball Game (continued)
Grammar, Usage, and Mechanics
Read each item. Fill in the correct answer.

1. In a sentence, the subject is
   - Ⓐ the action that a person or thing does.
   - Ⓑ the person or thing the sentence is about.
   - Ⓒ the words that describe a person or thing.
   - Ⓓ the word that links one thing to another.

2. Which word best describes the predicate of a sentence?
   - Ⓐ shape
   - Ⓑ thing
   - Ⓒ person
   - Ⓓ action

3. In which sentence is the predicate underlined?
   - Ⓐ The rabbit <u>ate</u> the green grass.
   - Ⓑ The rabbit ate the <u>green</u> grass.
   - Ⓒ The <u>rabbit</u> ate the green grass.
   - Ⓓ The rabbit ate the green <u>grass</u>.

4. In which sentence is the subject underlined?
   - Ⓐ The <u>red</u> car won the big race.
   - Ⓑ The red car won the big <u>race</u>.
   - Ⓒ The red <u>car</u> won the big race.
   - Ⓓ The red car <u>won</u> the big race.

5. Which of these words would probably be the subject of a sentence?
   - Ⓐ crawl
   - Ⓑ friend
   - Ⓒ happy
   - Ⓓ slowly

Grammar, Usage, and Mechanics • *Assessment 1*

A Cherokee Stickball Game (continued)

Analyzing the Selection

Read the question below. Write complete sentences for your answer. Support your answer with evidence from the selection.

Why do you think that Pretty Feathered Eagle was the coach of the Birds stickball team?

_____

_____

_____

_____

_____

_____

_____

_____

_____

_____

_____

_____

_____

_____

_____

_____

_____

_____

Teacher Directions: Duplicate this page for each student you choose to assess. Make one copy of the Unit 1 Lesson 4 Oral Fluency Assessment found on page 220 for students to read from.

A bat is a very unusual animal. It looks like a   1-11
mouse, but it flies like a bird. It has fur like an   12-23
animal but wings like a bird. Isn't that amazing?   24-32

Bats don't build nests like birds. They live in caves,   33-42
under bridges, and in other dark places. They do   43-51
this for protection. In a cave, bats are safe from bad   52-62
weather or animals that might eat them. Best of all,   63-72
the bats did not have to build their home. They just   73-83
moved right in.   84-86

Most bats eat flying insects. The bats come out   87-95
at night and fly around. When they find a tasty   96-105
flying bug, they gobble it up.   106-111

How do bats travel around at night, and how do   112-121
they find bugs? Bats make a squeaky noise. This   122-130
special noise bounces off a tree or bug. Bats hear   131-140
the echo of the sound. That way they can avoid   141-150
flying into trees and can also find food.   151-158

Evaluating Codes for Oral Fluency	
sky	(/) words read incorrectly
blue ^ sky	(^) Inserted word ([]) after the last word

Reading Rate and Accuracy	
Total Words Read	
Number of Errors	
Number of Correct Words Read per Minute (WCPM)	
Accuracy Rate	
(Number of Correct Words Read per Minute ÷ Total Words Read)	

Reading Prosody	LOW	AVG.	HIGH
Decoding Ability	○	○	○
Pace	○	○	○
Syntax	○	○	○
Self-correction	○	○	○
Intonation	○	○	○

Oral Fluency Passage Information	
Lexile Measure	560L
Mean Sentence Length	8.78
Mean Log Word Frequency	3.58
Word Count	158

Phonics: /er/ spelled *er, ir, ur*

Fill in the bubble under the correct spelling of each word.

1. dert   dirt   durt
    ◯   ◯   ◯

2. butter   buttur   buttor
    ◯   ◯   ◯

3. herry   hirry   hurry
    ◯   ◯   ◯

4. first   ferst   furst
    ◯   ◯   ◯

5. tertle   turtle   tirtle
    ◯   ◯   ◯

Phonics: /or/ spelled *or, ore*

Fill in the bubble under the correct spelling of each word.

6. fort   foort   foart
     ○   ○   ○

7. sor   soor   sore
     ○   ○   ○

8. boarn   born   boorn
     ○   ○   ○

9. stor   stoar   store
     ○   ○   ○

10. north   noorth   noarth
     ○   ○   ○

The Final Game
Vocabulary

Read each item. Fill in the correct answer.

1. What is a synonym for *tense* in this sentence? Do you feel a little *tense* before you take a test?
   Ⓐ anxious
   Ⓑ welcome
   Ⓒ thirsty
   Ⓓ smart

2. What does the word *commotion* mean in this sentence?
   The storm caused a *commotion* at doggy daycare.
   Ⓐ a flood
   Ⓑ a joyful sound
   Ⓒ a new idea
   Ⓓ a noisy confusion

3. What is a synonym for *piercing* in this sentence? The silence was followed by a *piercing* shout.
   Ⓐ grandstand
   Ⓑ loud
   Ⓒ dandy
   Ⓓ cabbage

4. What does the word *opponent* most likely mean in this sentence? My *opponent* in the game is really good.
   Ⓐ the field where a game is played
   Ⓑ cheers made by the fans
   Ⓒ someone who plays against you
   Ⓓ a meeting held before a game

5. What does the word *managed* mean in this sentence? My mother *managed* to get us tickets to the big game.
   Ⓐ called and told some friends
   Ⓑ checked the morning mail
   Ⓒ was able to do something
   Ⓓ let other people help out

The Final Game (continued)
Comprehension

Read the following items carefully and fill in the correct answer. You may look back at the selection to answer the questions.

1. The following question has two parts. First, answer **Part A**. Then, answer **Part B**.

   Part A What problem did Danny, Petou, and Anita face?
   - Ⓐ They were not very good players.
   - Ⓑ They joined the team late in the season.
   - Ⓒ They were blamed when the team lost.
   - Ⓓ They were late for the Bombers game.

   Part B Which sentence from the story **best** supports your answer for **Part A**?
   - Ⓐ Travis, who was our best forward, called us "the wimps" and said we weren't good enough to play on the team.
   - Ⓑ I arrived at the station late and out of breath.
   - Ⓒ I joined the team late in the season, along with my friends Petou and Anita.
   - Ⓓ At first Petou, Anita, and I played well and were part of the team.

2. Why did the cheering become a roar when Bob walked to the Wolves' bench?
   - Ⓐ Anita scored in a wild scramble.
   - Ⓑ He was coming home to rest an injured shoulder.
   - Ⓒ We were going into overtime.
   - Ⓓ They were excited to see a professional athlete at the game.

3. What inference can you make about Coach Matteau?
   - Ⓐ He played pro hockey.
   - Ⓒ He hates to lose.
   - Ⓑ He respects Bob.
   - Ⓓ He has a big family.

The Final Game (continued)
Comprehension

4. Why did Danny play goal?
- (A) His brother played goal, too.
- (B) He couldn't wear skates.
- (C) He was small but fast.
- (D) His friends were better players.

5. How do you know that Danny was nervous about the penalty shot?
- (A) Petou was off the ice.
- (C) He felt dizzy.
- (B) His opponent sneered.
- (D) Bob was in the stands.

Read the following items carefully. Answer the questions.

6. Who was most responsible for the win, Petou, Travis, or Bob? Support your answer with information from the story.

_____

7. Underline the words in this part of the story that show how Anita got hurt and had to leave the game.

    The second period was a battle. The Bombers tried to pick on Anita, roughing and tripping her without drawing a penalty. Finally they cross-checked her to the ice. She came to the bench fighting back tears. Travis yelled out, "What's the matter, wimp? Can't you take it?"

8. Why was Danny "tense and worried"?

_____

9. What do you think a "puck hog" is?

_____

10. What does it mean to be "torn between eagerness and fear"?

_____

The Final Game (continued)

Grammar, Usage, and Mechanics

Read each item. Fill in the correct answer.

1. Choose the sentence that has correct capitalization.
Ⓐ the team played together well.
Ⓑ The team played together well.
Ⓒ The Team played together well.
Ⓓ The team played together Well.

2. Choose the sentence that has correct capitalization.
Ⓐ our game will be on Friday after School.
Ⓑ Our Game will be on Friday after school.
Ⓒ Our game will be on Friday after school.
Ⓓ Our game will be on friday after school.

3. Choose the sentence that has correct capitalization.
Ⓐ My friend Petou scored the winning goal.
Ⓑ My friend petou scored the winning goal.
Ⓒ my friend Petou scored the winning goal.
Ⓓ my friend petou scored the winning goal.

4. Choose the sentence that has correct capitalization.
Ⓐ Many People in Canada enjoy hockey.
Ⓑ many people in Canada enjoy hockey.
Ⓒ Many people in canada enjoy hockey.
Ⓓ Many people in Canada enjoy hockey.

5. Choose the sentence that has correct capitalization.
Ⓐ The fans clapped for coach Matteau.
Ⓑ The fans clapped for Coach Matteau.
Ⓒ the fans clapped for coach matteau.
Ⓓ the fans clapped for Coach Matteau.

The Final Game (continued)
Analyzing the Selection

Read the question below. Write complete sentences for your answer. Support your answer with evidence from the selection.

How did Travis change in the story?

_____

_____

_____

_____

_____

_____

_____

_____

_____

_____

_____

_____

_____

_____

_____

_____

_____

_____

_____

_____

_____

_____

_____

Teacher Directions: Duplicate this page for each student you choose to assess. Make one copy of the Unit 1 Lesson 5 Oral Fluency Assessment found on page 221 for students to read from.

Ice hockey is a popular sport in many places.   1-9
Most of these places are cold, but some are warm.   10-19
You might be surprised to learn how many warm   20-28
places have hockey teams.   29-32

In places like Canada or the northern United   33-40
States, people like to play hockey outside. A frozen   41-49
pond or lake is perfect. A few friends show up with   50-60
skates, sticks, and a puck. The game is on.   61-69

Players in Canada may have invented ice hockey.   70-77
It is the country's national winter sport. Boys and   78-86
girls grow up playing hockey. Many of them dream   87-95
of becoming professional players. Even if they   96-102
don't become professionals, they will continue to   103-109
play as grown-ups.   110-112

Hockey has spread all over the world. Some of   113-121
the best players come from countries like Norway,   122-129
Sweden, and Finland. These are countries with cold   130-137
weather and lots of frozen ponds or lakes to play on.   138-148

But what about the rest of the world? How do   149-158
they play? The answer is easy. They play inside.   159-167
Ice arenas can be found all over the world.   168-176

Evaluating Codes for Oral Fluency

sky	(/) words read incorrectly
blue ^ sky	(^) Inserted word ([]) after the last word

Reading Rate and Accuracy

Total Words Read	
Number of Errors	
Number of Correct Words Read per Minute (WCPM)	
Accuracy Rate	
(Number of Correct Words Read per Minute ÷ Total Words Read)	

Reading Prosody

	LOW	AVG.	HIGH
Decoding Ability	○	○	○
Pace	○	○	○
Syntax	○	○	○
Self-correction	○	○	○
Intonation	○	○	○

Oral Fluency Passage Information

Lexile Measure	570L
Mean Sentence Length	8.80
Mean Log Word Frequency	3.56
Word Count	176

Name _____ Date _____ Score _____

Ellie's Long Walk
Vocabulary

Read each item. Fill in the correct answer.

1. What does the word *startled* mean in this sentence?
   The sound of the popping balloon *startled* Eli.
   - Ⓐ made calm
   - Ⓑ caused to move suddenly
   - Ⓒ knocked down
   - Ⓓ explained

2. What is a synonym for *panic* in this sentence? People felt *panic* when they saw the tornado.
   - Ⓐ fear
   - Ⓑ entire
   - Ⓒ inch
   - Ⓓ turn

3. What does the word *slick* most likely mean in this sentence? It was hard to walk on the *slick* trail.
   - Ⓐ outer
   - Ⓑ slippery
   - Ⓒ misty
   - Ⓓ removed

4. What does the word *slope* mean in this sentence? The skiers came down the *slope* quickly.
   - Ⓐ a deep mine
   - Ⓑ a tall roof
   - Ⓒ a kind of hill
   - Ⓓ a soft rock

5. What is a synonym for *journey* in this sentence? Everyone thought the *journey* would be easy.
   - Ⓐ trip
   - Ⓑ whistle
   - Ⓒ attack
   - Ⓓ face

Ellie's Long Walk (continued)
Comprehension

Read the following items carefully and fill in the correct answer. You may look back at the selection to answer the questions.

1. The following question has two parts. First, answer **Part A.** Then, answer **Part B.**

   Part A How did Ellie and Pam feel about starting the hike?
   - Ⓐ very tired
   - Ⓑ a little afraid
   - Ⓒ really happy
   - Ⓓ not quite ready

   Part B Which sentence from the story **best** supports your answer for **Part A**?
   - Ⓐ Each day Pam added small weights.
   - Ⓑ She was as excited as Pam to get started.
   - Ⓒ But Ellie had her own routine.
   - Ⓓ She was afraid one of the trees would smash them flat.

2. Which sentence moves the action forward in the story?
   - Ⓐ But Ellie had her own routine.
   - Ⓑ Pam carried Ellie's pack so it wouldn't get wet.
   - Ⓒ She was afraid one of the trees would smash them flat.
   - Ⓓ Together they entered the thick forest and began their hike south.

3. Which of these is an example of Ellie being silly?
   - Ⓐ Ellie would steal Pam's gloves.
   - Ⓑ Ellie was excited to see the snow.
   - Ⓒ Ellie helped Pam when she was hurt.
   - Ⓓ Ellie could smell other hikers.

Ellie's Long Walk (continued)
Comprehension

4. Where did Ellie and Pam live before the hike?
Ⓐ Maine　　　Ⓑ Georgia　　　Ⓒ Alaska　　　Ⓓ Connecticut

5. What made Pam think Ellie would be a good partner?
Ⓐ Ellie was black with a white chest.
Ⓑ Ellie liked to explore new places.
Ⓒ Ellie reached up with her tiny front paws.
Ⓓ Ellie let Pam pick her up right away.

Read the following items carefully. Answer the questions.

6. Why did Pam put an empty pack on Ellie the first day?

_____

7. Put these events in the order they happen in the story.
Use the numbers 1-4.

_____ Ellie sniffs around on the ice.

_____ Pam and Ellie walk for three hours every day.

_____ The crowd claps and cheers.

_____ Pam slips and smashes into a tree.

8. Which part of the journey seems most difficult to you?
Support your answer with evidence from the story.

_____

_____

9. How did Pam help Ellie?

_____

10. Why did the people in the parking lot clap and cheer?

_____

Ellie's Long Walk (continued)
Analyzing the Selection

Read the question below. Write complete sentences for your answer. Support your answer with evidence from the selection.

Why is the setting of this story so important?

_____

_____

_____

_____

_____

_____

_____

_____

_____

_____

_____

_____

_____

_____

Name _____ **Date** _____

Hiking is a wonderful activity. It is good exercise   1-9
and lets you enjoy nature in a very special way.   10-19
Best of all, you can hike almost anywhere,   20-27
including big cities.   28-30

When people think of hiking, they usually think   31-38
of forests and mountains. These are both good   39-46
places to hike. But there are lots of other options.   47-56
You can hike along beaches, beside rivers, and   57-64
on the shores of lakes. Some trails go through   65-73
swamps. Others take you through the desert. In   74-81
Hawaii, you can even hike near volcanoes.   82-88

When you hike, it is good to know where you   89-98
are. People often use their smart phones or other   99-107
electronic devices to follow a trail. Other people   108-115
like to do it the old-fashioned way. They use a   116-125
map made of paper. They think there is something   126-134
special about holding a map in their hand. The   135-143
people love figuring out where they are.   144-150

One of the most important parts of a hike is   151-160
looking up, down, and all around. There is always   161-169
something interesting to see. There are rocks on   170-177
the ground and birds in the sky. In between there   178-187
are trees, hills, and other wonderful sights.   188-194

Evaluating Codes for Oral Fluency	
sky	(/) words read incorrectly
blue ^ sky	(^) Inserted word ([]) after the last word

Reading Rate and Accuracy	
Total Words Read	
Number of Errors	
Number of Correct Words Read per Minute (WCPM)	
Accuracy Rate	
(Number of Correct Words Read per Minute ÷ Total Words Read)	

Reading Prosody	LOW	AVG.	HIGH
Decoding Ability	○	○	○
Pace	○	○	○
Syntax	○	○	○
Self-correction	○	○	○
Intonation	○	○	○

Oral Fluency Passage Information	
Lexile Measure	590L
Mean Sentence Length	9.70
Mean Log Word Frequency	3.69
Word Count	194

Phonics

Fill in the bubble under the correct spelling of each word.

1. lunsh   lunch   luntch
    ○   ○   ○

2. tchen   shen   then
    ○   ○   ○

3. wich   wish   wisch
    ○   ○   ○

4. white   wite   hwite
    ○   ○   ○

5. yord   jard   yard
    ○   ○   ○

Phonics

Look at the words in each group. Think about how the words are divided into syllables. Fill in the bubble under the word that has *closed* syllables.

6. circus   father   before
   ○   ○   ○

7. below   paper   after
   ○   ○   ○

8. tiger   follow   tiny
   ○   ○   ○

9. other   table   garden
   ○   ○   ○

10. around   summer   zero
    ○   ○   ○

Phonics

Fill in the bubble under the correct spelling of each word.

11. barrel   barrl   barril

        ○   ○   ○

12. drinck   drink   drinch

        ○   ○   ○

13. wronk   wrong   rwong

        ○   ○   ○

14. blink   blinch   blinct

        ○   ○   ○

15. troubel   troubl   trouble

        ○   ○   ○

Phonics

Fill in the bubble under the correct spelling of each word.

16. inchs   inchess   inches
     ○   ○   ○

17. elive   alive   ahlive
     ○   ○   ○

18. huntd   huntedd   hunted
     ○   ○   ○

19. boats   boates   boatses
     ○   ○   ○

20. pickng   picking   pickning
     ○   ○   ○

Phonics

Fill in the bubble under the correct spelling of each word.

21. thurd   third   thord
○   ○   ○

22. paper   papr   papre
○   ○   ○

23. stoar   store   stor
○   ○   ○

24. herd   hird   hiird
○   ○   ○

25. bern   buirn   burn
○   ○   ○

Name _____ **Date** _____ **Score** _____

Vocabulary

Read each item. Fill in the correct answer.

1. What does the word *surface* mean in this sentence?
   A lily pad floated on the *surface* of the pond.
   - Ⓐ the back side
   - Ⓑ the top part of something
   - Ⓒ the truth
   - Ⓓ an oily material

2. What is a synonym for *saddened* in this sentence?
   George was *saddened* because he lost the race.
   - Ⓐ consulted
   - Ⓑ descended
   - Ⓒ bordered
   - Ⓓ disappointed

3. What does the word *liquid* mean in this sentence?
   In the freezer, the juice went from a *liquid* to a solid.
   - Ⓐ not solid or gas
   - Ⓑ a bubble
   - Ⓒ something sharp
   - Ⓓ a reason

4. What is a synonym for *eagerness* in this sentence?
   The dog's *eagerness* to go for a walk made us laugh.
   - Ⓐ approach
   - Ⓑ voyage
   - Ⓒ enthusiasm
   - Ⓓ transferring

5. What does the word *entire* most likely mean in this sentence?
   The *entire* group of hikers made it to the top.
   - Ⓐ whole
   - Ⓑ tired
   - Ⓒ happy
   - Ⓓ first

Vocabulary

6. What is a synonym for *loyal* in this sentence? A *loyal* group of people took care of the park each weekend.
   - (A) thrifty
   - (B) dependable
   - (C) suggested
   - (D) retreating

7. What does the word *grandstand* mean in this sentence? People were in the *grandstand* waiting for the game.
   - (A) a place for people to sit
   - (B) a special kind of bus
   - (C) a group of people with team spirit
   - (D) a shelter near the stadium

8. What does the word *sneered* most likely mean in this sentence? A mean person *sneered* at the new players.
   - (A) tried to get in the way
   - (B) walked quickly
   - (C) tried to help
   - (D) said something unkind

9. What is a synonym for *protection* in this sentence? The hikers ran for the *protection* of the cave in the storm.
   - (A) entrance
   - (B) delivery
   - (C) safety
   - (D) cottage

10. What does the word *admired* mean in this sentence? Mya *admired* how strong her grandma was.
    - (A) watched
    - (B) pretended
    - (C) forgot
    - (D) really liked

Comprehension: Cold Read

Read the selection. Then answer the questions.

"The science fair isn't until May. It is only September. Why do you want to make a team and start now?" asked Vincent.

"Because the project will take a long time. It will be fun." Ada sighed as she answered. She even rolled her eyes. She knew it was not going to be easy to convince her friends to get involved in such a crazy project.

"Maybe it will help if you give everybody some details about the project." Their teacher, Mr. Hall, looked at Ada. "It is really a good idea, but it will take some explanation."

Instead of feeling upset, Ada smiled. She knew that her teacher was going to make this suggestion. She was ready. She opened the laptop computer on the desk and pressed a button. A slide show appeared on the screen. She pressed another button. Some pictures appeared on the screen. She talked while the pictures changed.

"The project is simple," said Ada. "We are going to take pictures in the park every day starting this week. We are going to show how plants and animals change over the period of nine months. When we are finished, we will have a great story."

"That sounds totally crazy. I love the idea," whispered Reese. She whispered, but it was loud enough for everyone to hear. The rest of the team laughed. They were beginning to understand. This was a pretty great idea.

"How are we going to take all the pictures?" asked Sergio. "We can't sit in the park all day. Maybe Principal Brooks will let us skip school."

Comprehension: Cold Read

Everyone laughed. Mr. Hall said, "Ms. Brooks is not going to do that. But there is a way to solve the problem. Would you explain, Harish?"

"My parents work for a company that makes a special kind of camera. It works automatically. It is also meant for use outdoors. The company has donated some cameras to our class. We are going to set them up around the park. They will take pictures every minute of every day. We will visit the cameras every few days and change the memory. We will load the pictures into a computer and arrange them in order. Not all the pictures will be used because we will have so many. But we will pick the best ones for each day."

"There's one more thing," added Mr. Hall. "We will all visit the park and take some of our own pictures. There will be lots of things that the fixed cameras will miss. We want to be sure to take pictures of these things."

Harish opened a box. He pulled out what looked like a plastic box. This was the camera. It had a strap on the back. The strap could wrap around a tree. There were other ways to set up the camera. He showed everyone how it worked.

"Now it is all making sense," said Vincent. "Let's get started. Those cameras aren't going to set themselves up."

Comprehension

Read the following items. You may look back at the selection to answer the questions.

1. Which of these inferences can you make about the story?
   - (A) Mr. Hall thinks the project is too hard for the class.
   - (B) Reese is shy.
   - (C) Ada discussed her idea with her teacher first.
   - (D) Sergio doesn't like doing school projects very much.

2. How often will the automatic cameras take pictures?
   - (A) every minute of everyday
   - (B) every hour
   - (C) every few days
   - (D) once a week

3. Which sentence shows how long the project will take?
   - (A) We are going to show how plants and animals change over the period of nine months.
   - (B) The science fair isn't until May.
   - (C) We will visit the cameras every few days.
   - (D) We can't sit in the park all day.

4. Which of these **best** explains the main idea of the passage?
   - (A) Some cameras take pictures without pressing a button.
   - (B) A girl convinces students to get started on a project.
   - (C) Talk to a teacher before starting a science project.
   - (D) A science project is a lot of fun.

5. If this story was a fable, how might it have been different?
   - (A) The author would inform the reader about cameras.
   - (B) The girl would persuade her friends to help.
   - (C) Instead of people, the characters would have been animals.
   - (D) The team would not have laughed at what Ada said.

Grammar, Usage, and Mechanics

Read each item. Fill in the correct answer.

1. Complete the sentence using a common noun.
I finally learned how to tie my _____.
Ⓐ Friday   Ⓒ kick
Ⓑ shoes   Ⓓ which

2. Complete the sentence using a proper noun.
_____ is the eighth month of the year.
Ⓐ birthday   Ⓒ August
Ⓑ warm   Ⓓ swim

3. Read the story below. Circle the best action verb for each sentence.
The first Arbor Day **happened/are** in 1872. Every year at the end of April, Arbor Day **are/is** celebrated. People around the globe **plant/put** trees to **use/help** Earth.

4. Which helping verb completes this sentence?
My sister _____ play the piano.
Ⓐ am   Ⓒ can
Ⓑ is   Ⓓ do

5. Which linking verb completes this sentence?
The trees in the forest _____ very tall.
Ⓐ are   Ⓒ is
Ⓑ am   Ⓓ was

Grammar, Usage, and Mechanics

6. Complete the sentence using a predicate.
A small plane _____ at the airport.
- (A) blue
- (B) landed
- (C) are
- (D) Friday

7. Choose the subject that completes the sentence.
A big _____ crashed against the shore.
- (A) train
- (B) cat
- (C) wave
- (D) school

8. Choose the subject and predicate that complete the sentence.
A big gray _____ in the pond in the park.
- (A) they are
- (B) cloud came
- (C) goose swam
- (D) school is

Triple-underline the letters that should be capital letters.
Rewrite the sentences.

9. Thanksgiving is the last Thursday in november.

_____

_____

10. This summer i went to texas to visit family.

_____

_____

Spelling

Choose the correct way to spell the underlined word. If the underlined word is correct, choose the last answer, *Leave as is.* Fill in the correct answer.

1. Some friends will <u>marth</u> in the parade.
   Ⓐ martch
   Ⓑ marsh
   Ⓒ march
   Ⓓ Leave as is.

2. Birds made their nests in the old <u>shed</u>.
   Ⓐ ched
   Ⓑ thed
   Ⓒ sched
   Ⓓ Leave as is.

3. It will be hard to <u>juge</u> which tastes better.
   Ⓐ judge
   Ⓑ juje
   Ⓒ judje
   Ⓓ Leave as is.

4. The train <u>trak</u> goes beside our school.
   Ⓐ trac
   Ⓑ trackt
   Ⓒ track
   Ⓓ Leave as is.

5. The fans <u>clappd</u> for the winning team.
   Ⓐ clappded
   Ⓑ clapped
   Ⓒ clappted
   Ⓓ Leave as is.

Spelling

6. Jan <u>wishs</u> she could be here.
   - (A) wishss
   - (B) wishes
   - (C) wishdes
   - (D) Leave as is.

7. Some cows are in the <u>middel</u> of the field.
   - (A) middle
   - (B) middell
   - (C) middl
   - (D) Leave as is.

8. The wet pants <u>shrank</u> when they dried.
   - (A) shranch
   - (B) shranc
   - (C) shranck
   - (D) Leave as is.

9. Let's do our <u>choores</u> now.
   - (A) choars
   - (B) choors
   - (C) chores
   - (D) Leave as is.

10. This <u>porple</u> flower is very pretty.
    - (A) parple
    - (B) purple
    - (C) perpel
    - (D) Leave as is.

Teacher Directions: Duplicate this page for each student you choose to assess. Make one copy of the Unit 1 Oral Fluency Assessment found on page 223 for students to read from.

Long ago, people ate only raw food. Cooking had to wait until people learned to use fire. But it was a great idea. It makes many kinds of food safer by killing germs. Cooking also makes food easier for your body to use.

When you digest food, you turn it into something that your body can use. After you eat food, it goes to your stomach. Here and in other parts of your body it is turned into energy. The food is used by your body to make you strong and smart.

Cooking allowed people to eat more and different things. People did not starve because they had many things to eat.

Here's a surprising thing about cooking. It helped to make people smarter. People sat around the cooking fire. They talked to each other. They learned from one another. They became friends. They learned to share food. All of this helped to make people into a strong tribe.

Probably the best thing about cooking is that it made food taste better. At first, people just put meat in a fire and let it burn. After a while, people learned how to make pots. They could mix different foods together and cook them. The food tasted wonderful, and the world was changed forever.

1-9	
10-20	
21-31	
32-39	
40-43	
44-52	
53-63	
64-73	
74-84	
85-92	
93-100	
101-108	
109-112	
113-120	
121-128	
129-136	
137-143	
144-153	
154-159	
160-168	
169-177	
178-189	
190-198	
199-206	
207-213	

Evaluating Codes for Oral Fluency

sky	(/) words read incorrectly
blue ^ sky	(^) Inserted word ([]) after the last word

Reading Rate and Accuracy

Total Words Read	
Number of Errors	
Number of Correct Words Read per Minute (WCPM)	
Accuracy Rate	
(Number of Correct Words Read per Minute ÷ Total Words Read)	

Reading Prosody

	LOW	AVG.	HIGH
Decoding Ability	○	○	○
Pace	○	○	○
Syntax	○	○	○
Self-correction	○	○	○
Intonation	○	○	○

Oral Fluency Passage Information

Lexile Measure	510L
Mean Sentence Length	8.88
Mean Log Word Frequency	3.73
Word Count	213

Opinion Writing Task

Imagine that your school allowed students to bring pets to the classroom. Do you think this is a good idea or not? Write your opinion. When you write, remember to

- include at least two reasons that support your opinion clearly.
- use correct grammar, spelling, punctuation, and capitalization.

_____

_____

_____

_____

_____

_____

_____

_____

_____

_____

_____

_____

_____

_____

_____

_____

_____

_____

Four Point Rubrics for Persuasive and Opinion Writing

Genre	1 Point	2 Points	3 Points	4 Points
Persuasive and Opinion Writing	Position is absent or confusing. Insufficient writing to show that criteria are met.	Position is vague or lacks clarity. Unrelated ideas or multiple positions are included.	An opening statement identifies position. Writing may develop fewer or more points than delineated in opening. Focus may be too broad.	Sets scope and purpose of paper in introduction. Maintains position throughout. Supports arguments. Includes effective closing.
Writing Traits				
Audience	Displays little or no sense of audience.	Displays some sense of audience.	Writes with audience in mind throughout.	Displays a strong sense of audience. Engages audience.
Focus	Topic is unclear or wanders and must be inferred. Extraneous material may be present.	Topic/position/direction is unclear and must be inferred.	Topic/position is stated and direction/purpose is previewed and maintained. Mainly stays on topic.	Topic/position is clearly stated, previewed, and maintained throughout the paper. Topics and details are tied together with a central theme or purpose that is maintained/threaded throughout the paper.
Organization	The writing lacks coherence; organization seems haphazard and disjointed. Plan is not evident. Facts are presented randomly. No transitions are included. Beginning is weak and ending is abrupt. There is no awareness of paragraph structure or organization.	An attempt has been made to organize the writing; however, the overall structure is inconsistent or skeletal. Plan is evident but loosely structured or writer overuses a particular pattern. Writing may be a listing of facts/ideas with a weak beginning or conclusion. Transitions are awkward or nonexistent. Includes beginning use of paragraphs.	Organization is clear and coherent. Order and structure are present, but may seem formulaic. Plan is evident. Reasons for order of key concepts may be unclear. Beginning or conclusion is included but may lack impact. Transitions are present. Paragraph use is appropriate.	The organization enhances the central idea and its development. The order and structure are compelling and move the reader through the text easily. Plan is evident. Key concepts are logically sequenced. Beginning grabs attention. Conclusion adds impact. Uses a variety of transitions that enhance meaning. Uses paragraphs appropriately.
Writing Conventions				
Conventions Overall	Numerous errors in usage, grammar, spelling, capitalization, and punctuation repeatedly distract the reader and make the text difficult to read. The reader finds it difficult to focus on the message.	The writing demonstrates limited control of standard writing conventions (punctuation, spelling, grammar, and usage). Errors sometimes impede readability.	The writing demonstrates control of standard writing conventions (punctuation, spelling, grammar, and usage). Minor errors, while perhaps noticeable, do not impede readability.	The writing demonstrates exceptionally strong control of standard writing conventions (punctuation, spelling, grammar, and usage) and uses them effectively to enhance communication. Errors are so few and so minor that the reader can easily skim over them.

Phonics: /ā/ spelled *a, a_e*

Read the following words. Underline the *a* or *a_e* spelling pattern used in each word. Write the word on the line.

1. cave _____

2. gate _____

3. April _____

4. game _____

5. able _____

Phonics: /ī/ spelled *i*, *i_e*

Circle the correct spelling of each word.

6. rice   ric

7. thriv   thrive

8. side   sid

9. kind   kinde

10. like   lik

Name _____ **Date** _____ **Score** _____

Mattland

Vocabulary

Read each item. Fill in the correct answer.

1. What does the word *prickly* most likely mean in this sentence?
    The plant had *prickly* leaves that hurt.
    - Ⓐ large
    - Ⓑ spiky
    - Ⓒ round
    - Ⓓ smooth

2. What is a synonym for *peaks* in this sentence?
    The *peaks* of the mountains were covered with trees.
    - Ⓐ tops
    - Ⓑ sides
    - Ⓒ rocks
    - Ⓓ farms

3. What does the word *culvert* mean in this sentence?
    When the *culvert* filled with leaves, the road flooded.
    - Ⓐ a large pond
    - Ⓑ a wooded trail
    - Ⓒ a new market
    - Ⓓ a drain for water

4. What is a synonym for *jagged* in this sentence?
    The edge of the rock was *jagged*.
    - Ⓐ heavy
    - Ⓑ careful
    - Ⓒ rough
    - Ⓓ early

5. What does the word *pasture* mean in this sentence?
    Horses and cows were in the *pasture*.
    - Ⓐ shade
    - Ⓑ night
    - Ⓒ meadow
    - Ⓓ parade

Mattland (continued)

Comprehension

Read the following items carefully and fill in the correct answer. You may look back at the selection to answer the questions.

1. The following question has two parts. First, answer **Part A**. Then, answer **Part B**.

   Part A What did Matt do with the first thing that the outsider gave him?
   - (A) He saved it.
   - (B) He threw it away.
   - (C) He used it.
   - (D) He gave it back.

   Part B Which sentence from the story **best** supports your answer for **Part A**?
   - (A) An outsider had arrived in Mattland.
   - (B) Finally, she reached out a hand.
   - (C) The stick became fence posts for Burr-Berry farm.
   - (D) At Snake River something larger was needed.

2. How did Matt choose names for the places he made?
   - (A) He made them up.
   - (B) He used real names.
   - (C) He asked the outsider.
   - (D) He used a list.

3. What caused Matt and the outsider to work together?
   - (A) The water calmed.
   - (B) The outsider filled both her hands.
   - (C) Matt felt lonely.
   - (D) A rainstorm began.

Mattland (continued)

Comprehension

4. Read this sentence from the story.
   The leftover bits made an interesting pattern on the earth, and soon the Pine Needle Railway Line raced across the flats. What is the phrase "the flats" describing?
   - (A) how Matt felt about the place
   - (B) the pattern that the leftover bits made
   - (C) an area of ground that is smooth
   - (D) the railroad tracks

5. Why do you think that fuzzy seeds became sheep in the pasture?
   - (A) The seeds were on his sock.
   - (B) Sheep are fuzzy like the seeds.
   - (C) Some socks are made of sheep wool.
   - (D) The wind blew the seeds around.

Read the following items carefully. Use complete sentences to answer the questions.

6. How did the stick help Matt at the beginning of the story?

   _____

7. What was Matt's first reaction to the outsider?

   _____

8. Why do you think the outsider came to Matt?

   _____

9. Why did Matt think his new home was the worst place of all?

   _____

10. What do you think the setting is for this story?

    _____

Mattland (continued)

Grammar, Usage, and Mechanics

Read each item. Circle the word group that correctly completes each sentence. Rewrite the complete sentence on the line below.

1. Rivers   flow from the Rocky Mountains.
            with boats and barges.

_____

2. People   parks out west.
            stopped to watch the bears.

_____

3. Albert   after waking up.
            opened his eyes.

_____

4. Rewrite this sentence fragment to make it a complete sentence.
To the library.

_____

5. Rewrite this sentence fragment to make it a complete sentence.
After school?

_____

Mattland (continued)

Analyzing the Selection

Read the question below. Write complete sentences for your answer. Support your answer with evidence from the selection.

How do you think Matt's feelings about the outsider changed in the story?

_____

_____

_____

_____

_____

_____

_____

_____

_____

_____

_____

_____

_____

_____

_____

_____

_____

Teacher Directions: Duplicate this page for each student you choose to assess. Make one copy of the Unit 2 Lesson 1 Oral Fluency Assessment found on page 224 for students to read from.

A group of people stood around a puddle on the ground. From the puddle spilled a small stream of water. The puddle and stream had come from nowhere. During the night, a spring had appeared in the park, and no one knew what had caused it.	1-10 11-18 19-27 28-35 36-46
The stream flowed through the park. It ran down the slope and between trees, soon joining up with another stream.	47-55 56-64 65-66
The park ranger walked up to the group. She looked at the spring and said, "Welcome back." The people were curious. They asked her what she was talking about.	67-75 76-83 84-92 93-95
"A long time ago, there was a spring here," she said. "Then we had many dry years. This year we have had a lot of rain and snow. Some people thought the spring had dried up, but others thought it was sleeping. I guess they were right. The spring was taking a nap. It was waiting for the rain."	96-105 106-114 115-125 126-134 135-144 145-154

Evaluating Codes for Oral Fluency

sky	(/) words read incorrectly
blue ^ sky	(^) Inserted word ([]) after the last word

Reading Rate and Accuracy

Total Words Read	
Number of Errors	
Number of Correct Words Read per Minute (WCPM)	
Accuracy Rate	
(Number of Correct Words Read per Minute ÷ Total Words Read)	

Reading Prosody

	LOW	AVG.	HIGH
Decoding Ability	○	○	○
Pace	○	○	○
Syntax	○	○	○
Self-correction	○	○	○
Intonation	○	○	○

Oral Fluency Passage Information

Lexile Measure	440L
Mean Sentence Length	9.06
Mean Log Word Frequency	3.94
Word Count	154

Name _____ **Date** _____ **Score** _____

Phonics: /ō/ spelled o, o_e

Read each sentence. Circle the word that best completes the sentence.

1. The dog chewed its _____.

bon   bone

2. I _____ to go to the zoo tomorrow.

hope   hop

3. I ate _____ of the food on my plate.

mots   most

4. My dad told a funny _____.

joke   jok

5. It was _____ outside.

cowd   cold

Phonics: /ū/ spelled *u, u_e*

Read each sentence. Circle the word that best completes the sentence.

6. The soldier played the _____ at the ceremony.

bugle   bugol

7. The leaves on the plant were _____.

uge   huge

8. The _____ carried a heavy pack on its back.

mule   mul

9. My dad joined a _____ at work.

uneon   union

10. We handled the situation the _____ way.

usual   useual

A River of Ice

Vocabulary

Read each item. Fill in the correct answer.

1. What is a synonym for *over* in this sentence?
The puppy grew quickly *over* a few months.
- Ⓐ outside
- Ⓑ than
- Ⓒ while
- Ⓓ during

2. What does the word *crevasse* mean in this sentence?
The *crevasse* in the canyon wall formed many years ago.
- Ⓐ a river
- Ⓑ a deep crack
- Ⓒ a motor
- Ⓓ a nuisance

3. What is a synonym for *press* in this sentence?
You had to *press* a big button to open the door.
- Ⓐ show
- Ⓑ push
- Ⓒ find
- Ⓓ ring

4. What does the word *fjord* most likely mean in this sentence?
The boat sailed into the *fjord*.
- Ⓐ a deep inlet
- Ⓑ a small island
- Ⓒ a big dock
- Ⓓ a frozen lake

5. What does the word *glacier* mean in this sentence?
A *glacier* filled the valley between the mountains.
- Ⓐ river of ice
- Ⓑ small forest
- Ⓒ pile of rocks
- Ⓓ long lake

A River of Ice (continued)

Comprehension

Read the following items carefully and fill in the correct answer. You may look back at the selection to answer the questions.

1. The following question has two parts. First, answer **Part A.** Then, answer **Part B.**

Part A Where are glaciers most likely to form?
- Ⓐ anywhere that it snows
- Ⓑ in high places that are cold
- Ⓒ only near the North Pole
- Ⓓ where there are not many trees

Part B Which sentence from the article **best** supports your answer for **Part A**?
- Ⓐ Water moves into the snow and freezes.
- Ⓑ Glaciers covered large parts of the world during the last ice age.
- Ⓒ Valleys made by glaciers are found around the world.
- Ⓓ Sometimes snow that is high up in the mountains does not melt.

2. Why did the author write this article?
- Ⓐ to inform the reader about glaciers
- Ⓑ to convince the reader that crevasses are dangerous
- Ⓒ to entertain the reader
- Ⓓ to express an opinion about glaciers

A River of Ice (continued)
Comprehension

3. Which answer would be the best caption to go with a picture of a fjord?
   - (A) This bay is shallow and has a sandy bottom.
   - (B) Some words we use have strange spellings.
   - (C) This fjord was formed by a large glacier.
   - (D) Many glaciers are getting smaller each year.

4. What does the author say about the northern states long ago?
   - (A) They were covered in ice.
   - (B) They had no lakes at all.
   - (C) They were covered with rock flour.
   - (D) They had many crevasses.

5. About how much of Earth is covered with glaciers today?
   - (A) more than half
   - (B) more than a quarter
   - (C) ten percent
   - (D) five percent

Read the following items carefully. Use complete sentences to answer the questions.

6. How are fjords made?

   _____

7. Are there more or fewer glaciers than long ago?

   _____

8. What is rock flour, and how is it made?

   _____

9. Why is a crevasse dangerous?

   _____

10. How do glaciers form?

   _____

A River of Ice (continued)

Grammar, Usage, and Mechanics

Read each item. Fill in the correct answer.

1. Which of these sentences is interrogative?
Ⓐ Tell me all about your trip.
Ⓑ Did you say something to me?
Ⓒ Wow, what a great rainbow.
Ⓓ The picture you sent is very pretty.

2. Which of these sentences is declarative?
Ⓐ Quick, take a picture of the snake on the boulder!
Ⓑ Tell me what you know about this boulder.
Ⓒ What is this boulder made of?
Ⓓ This boulder is made of granite.

3. Which of these sentences is imperative?
Ⓐ Let the soup cool before eating it.
Ⓑ What are we having for lunch?
Ⓒ The soup was made with our vegetables.
Ⓓ Don't spill your soup on your new pants!

4. Which of these sentences is exclamatory?
Ⓐ The waves crashed against the rocks.
Ⓑ How far did these waves travel?
Ⓒ Watch out, a big wave is coming in!
Ⓓ Take your shoes off before going in the water.

5. Which of these sentences has correct punctuation?
Ⓐ The next stop on this train is Los Angeles!
Ⓑ Can we visit the museum on Saturday?
Ⓒ Be sure to close the door when you come in?
Ⓓ How do you open this kind of package.

Grammar, Usage, and Mechanics • *Assessment 1*

A River of Ice (continued)

Analyzing the Selection

Read the question below. Write complete sentences for your answer. Support your answer with evidence from the selection.

What are some ways that glaciers change the land?

_____

_____

_____

_____

_____

_____

_____

_____

_____

_____

_____

_____

_____

_____

_____

_____

_____

Teacher Directions: Duplicate this page for each student you choose to assess. Make one copy of the Unit 2 Lesson 2 Oral Fluency Assessment found on page 225 for students to read from.

The lake was long and deep. It looked like it	1-10
could have been made by humans. But that is not	11-20
how it was made. A glacier did it.	21-28
Thousands of years ago, the area was covered	29-36
by ice. It was hundreds of feet thick in spots. The	37-47
weight of the ice was great. It pressed down on the	48-58
ground so hard that it cut a big hole.	59-67
The ice grew thicker because Earth was colder	68-75
than the ice. Earth started to warm up, and the	76-85
giant ice sheet melted. Eventually, it disappeared.	86-92
It left behind gashes in the ground. Sometimes	93-100
they filled with water and became lakes.	101-107
Around the lake there were also big rocks called	108-116
boulders. These rocks looked different from the	117-123
other rocks in the area. That's because they were	124-132
different. They were brought to the area by the	133-141
glaciers from places far away. The rocks got stuck	142-150
in the glacier. They moved when the glacier moved.	151-159
When it melted, they stayed where they were	160-167
dropped.	168

Evaluating Codes for Oral Fluency

sky	(/) words read incorrectly
blue ^ sky	(^) Inserted word ([]) after the last word

Reading Rate and Accuracy

Total Words Read	
Number of Errors	
Number of Correct Words Read per Minute (WCPM)	
Accuracy Rate	
(Number of Correct Words Read per Minute ÷ Total Words Read)	

Reading Prosody

	LOW	AVG.	HIGH
Decoding Ability	○	○	○
Pace	○	○	○
Syntax	○	○	○
Self-correction	○	○	○
Intonation	○	○	○

Oral Fluency Passage Information

Lexile Measure	440L
Mean Sentence Length	8.30
Mean Log Word Frequency	3.78
Word Count	168

Phonics: /ā/ spelled *a*, /ī/ spelled *i*, /ō/ spelled *o* and /ū/ spelled *u*, *u_e*

Fill in the bubble under the correct spelling of each word.

1. beasic   baisic   basic
○   ○   ○

2. eitems   items   aitems
○   ○   ○

3. usful   uusful   useful
○   ○   ○

4. music   museic   muusic
○   ○   ○

5. poast   post   poest
○   ○   ○

Phonics: Inflectional Endings *–er* and *–est*

Read each sentence. Choose the word that best completes the sentence.

6. Jen has the _____ hair in the class.

   longest   longer   long

    ○   ○   ○

7. Bob lives _____ to school than Lisa.

   near   nearer   nearest

    ○   ○   ○

8. A robin is _____ than a finch.

   biggest   big   bigger

    ○   ○   ○

9. Ms. Gomez is the _____ person I know.

   kindest   kind   kinder

    ○   ○   ○

10. The music is _____ than before.

   loud   loudest   louder

    ○   ○   ○

Phonics: /n/ spelled *kn_*, *gn* and /r/ spelled *wr_*

Choose a word from the box below to complete each sentence. Write the word on the line.

knot	wrist	knob	wrap	sign

11. I turned the door _____ to enter the house.

12. I hurt my _____ playing basketball.

13. My shoestring is tied in a _____.

14. Joe needs to _____ the gift he bought.

15. He made a _____ for the lemonade stand.

What Makes the Earth Shake?
Vocabulary

Read each item. Fill in the correct answer.

1. What does the word *aloft* mean in this sentence? The leaf was held *aloft* by the breeze.
- (A) in a twisted way
- (B) behind
- (C) far above the ground
- (D) nervously

2. What is a synonym for *spied* in this sentence? The hikers *spied* an eagle in a tall tree.
- (A) saw
- (B) reported
- (C) swarmed
- (D) drew

3. What does the word *settled* most likely mean in this sentence? The sinking boat *settled* on the bottom of the lake.
- (A) broke into pieces
- (B) moved quickly
- (C) floated above
- (D) came to rest

4. What does the word *shivers* mean in this sentence? My dog *shivers* when we walk in the cold.
- (A) drifts
- (B) barks
- (C) shakes
- (D) pulls

5. What is a synonym for *restless* in this sentence? The *restless* lion walked back and forth in the cage.
- (A) moving
- (B) beautiful
- (C) great
- (D) real

What Makes the Earth Shake? (continued)

Comprehension

Read the following items carefully and fill in the correct answer. You may look back at the selection to answer the questions.

1. The following question has two parts. First, answer **Part A.** Then, answer **Part B.**

   Part A One difference between people today and long ago is that
   Ⓐ people today have better myths about earthquakes.
   Ⓑ people long ago understood earthquakes better.
   Ⓒ people today know what causes earthquakes.
   Ⓓ people long ago didn't have real earthquakes.

   Part B Which sentence from the selection **best** supports your answer for **Part A**?
   Ⓐ It now had beautiful land too.
   Ⓑ Long ago, humans did not know what caused earthquakes.
   Ⓒ But sometimes the turtles still grow restless, and then Earth shakes again.
   Ⓓ The land shakes and rolls.

2. What do all the earthquake myths have in common?
   Ⓐ They all show that people knew Earth was round.
   Ⓑ They all involve special people that are not humans.
   Ⓒ They all blame earthquakes on turtles.
   Ⓓ They all show that Earth was at one time made only of water.

3. How is Namazu different from Kwawar?
   Ⓐ Kwawar does not cause earthquakes.
   Ⓑ Namazu lives in the sky.
   Ⓒ Kwawar is held down by a stone.
   Ⓓ Namazu has to guard a giant catfish.

Comprehension

4. In the West African story, what are the trees?
- Ⓐ the elephant's tail
- Ⓒ the catfish's whiskers
- Ⓑ the turtle's claws
- Ⓓ the giant's hair

5. In which two stories are east and west mentioned?
- Ⓐ Native American and West African
- Ⓑ Japanese and West African
- Ⓒ West African and Indian
- Ⓓ Indian and Japanese

Read the following items carefully. Use complete sentences to answer the questions.

6. What happens when Kashima leaves his place?

_____

_____

7. How does the West African giant cause earthquakes?

_____

_____

8. Describe how the animals stack up in the Indian myth.

_____

_____

9. How did Kwawar make Earth?

_____

_____

10. Why do you think so many of the earthquake myths were based on animals?

_____

_____

Comprehension • *Assessment 1*

What Makes the Earth Shake? (continued)
Grammar, Usage, and Mechanics

Read each item. Fill in the correct answer.

1. Which of these is not a proper noun, even though it begins with a capital letter?
   Ⓐ Miami　Ⓑ Which　Ⓒ Colorado　Ⓓ Roberta

2. Which sentence has correct capitalization?
   Ⓐ Vijay asked a question about the Grand canyon?
   Ⓑ vijay asked a question about the grand Canyon.
   Ⓒ Vijay asked a question about the Grand Canyon.
   Ⓓ Vijay asked a question about the grand canyon.

3. Which sentence has correct capitalization?
   Ⓐ The family played a board game called Smart Sayings.
   Ⓑ The Family played a board game called Smart Sayings.
   Ⓒ The family played a board game called smart sayings.
   Ⓓ The family played a Board Game called Smart Sayings.

4. Which sentence has correct capitalization?
   Ⓐ The Mississippi river flows through many states.
   Ⓑ The mississippi river flows through many states.
   Ⓒ The Mississippi River flows through many states.
   Ⓓ The Mississippi River flows through many States.

5. Which sentence has correct capitalization?
   Ⓐ italy is a country with many beaches.
   Ⓑ Italy is a Country with many beaches.
   Ⓒ Italy is a country with many beaches.
   Ⓓ Italy is a country with many Beaches.

What Makes the Earth Shake? (continued)
Analyzing the Selection

Read the question below. Write complete sentences for your answer. Support your answer with evidence from the selection.

Compare two of the earthquake myths that you read. Summarize the myths. Decide which one you like best and explain why.

_____

_____

_____

_____

_____

_____

_____

_____

_____

_____

_____

_____

_____

_____

_____

_____

_____

_____

Analyzing the Selection • *Assessment 1*

Name _____ **Date** _____

It was Claude's first visit to California. He was staying with his cousins who were about his age. He was having a great time visiting places he had never been.	1-9 10-18 19-28 29-30
One day they were in a forest near the Pacific Ocean. All of a sudden, the ground began to shake. It shook so hard that they all fell over.	31-40 41-49 50-59
"What was that?" asked Claude while he was still on the ground.	60-67 68-71
"That was a little earthquake called a tremor," answered Aunt Lillian. "Why don't we all stay on the ground for a few minutes to make sure it's over."	72-79 80-87 88-97 98-99
Claude had no problem with that. In fact, he was afraid to get up. He was also amazed that everyone else seemed so calm.	100-108 109-118 119-123
Uncle Phil noticed the look on Claude's face. He said, "We're used to it. Tremors happen here pretty often. They don't cause damage. We are in a safe place here. There are no buildings around. Your cousin Veronica will tell you all about the geology here."	124-131 132-140 141-149 150-158 159-167 168-169

Evaluating Codes for Oral Fluency

sky	(/) words read incorrectly
blue ^ sky	(^) Inserted word (]) after the last word

Reading Rate and Accuracy

Total Words Read	
Number of Errors	
Number of Correct Words Read per Minute (WCPM)	
Accuracy Rate	
(Number of Correct Words Read per Minute ÷ Total Words Read)	

Reading Prosody

	LOW	AVG.	HIGH
Decoding Ability	○	○	○
Pace	○	○	○
Syntax	○	○	○
Self-correction	○	○	○
Intonation	○	○	○

Oral Fluency Passage Information

Lexile Measure	460L
Mean Sentence Length	8.89
Mean Log Word Frequency	3.86
Word Count	169

Phonics: /ē/ spelled e, e_e

Write the long-vowel spelling pattern for each word on the line.

1. evening _____

2. equal _____

3. these _____

4. me _____

5. even _____

Phonics • *Assessment 1*

Phonics: Review /ā/, /ē/, /ī/, /ō/, /ū/

Unscramble the following letters. Underline the spelling pattern in each word. Write each new word on the line.

6. b a f l e _____

7. n i k d _____

8. n s e o _____

9. e e v _____

10. u i n t _____

All about Earthquakes

Vocabulary

Read each item. Fill in the correct answer.

1. What does the word *structures* most likely mean in this sentence?
   Structures lined the banks of the river.
   (A) cliffs   (C) buildings
   (B) storms   (D) animals

2. What is the meaning of *absorb* in this sentence?
   A sponge will *absorb* water.
   (A) freeze   (C) soak up
   (B) make warm   (D) handle

3. What does the word *boundaries* mean in this sentence?
   We have a fence along the *boundaries* of our yard.
   (A) arches   (C) the highest points
   (B) the edges of   (D) rocky areas
       something

4. What is a synonym for *collide* in this sentence?
   Be careful or you will *collide* with that bike.
   (A) pass   (C) store
   (B) lose   (D) crash

5. What does the word *energy* mean in this sentence?
   Some of our *energy* comes from the sun.
   (A) power   (C) signals
   (B) record   (D) worries

All about Earthquakes (continued)
Comprehension

Read the following items carefully and fill in the correct answer. You may look back at the selection to answer the questions.

1. The following question has two parts. First, answer **Part A**. Then, answer **Part B**.

   Part A How well do Earth's plates fit together?
   - Ⓐ close together
   - Ⓑ not very well
   - Ⓒ with a lot of space in between
   - Ⓓ loosely most of the time

   Part B Which sentence from the article **best** supports your answer for **Part A**?
   - Ⓐ Earth's surface, or crust, is made up of many plates.
   - Ⓑ Plates usually fit tightly together.
   - Ⓒ Plates can move away from each other.
   - Ⓓ As they do, they rub against each other.

2. What is one effect of a tsunami mentioned in the selection?
   - Ⓐ It can wash away buildings.
   - Ⓑ It can cause rivers to move.
   - Ⓒ It can wash mountains away.
   - Ⓓ It can cause islands to form.

3. How do scientists try to guess when earthquakes will happen?
   - Ⓐ by measuring how rivers move
   - Ⓑ by looking for tsunamis
   - Ⓒ by seeing how buildings sway
   - Ⓓ by watching plate movements

Comprehension

4. You can infer from the story that most earthquakes
   Ⓐ cause a lot of damage in big cities.
   Ⓑ happen where plates come together.
   Ⓒ create giant waves called tsunamis.
   Ⓓ make new mountain ranges.

5. All of Earth's plates make up the
   Ⓐ orbit.   Ⓒ crust.
   Ⓑ desert.   Ⓓ core.

Read the following items carefully. Use complete sentences to answer the questions.

6. How do Earth's plates cause earthquakes?

   _____

   _____

7. How are seismic waves and tsunamis alike? How are they different?

   _____

   _____

8. In what ways do plates interact?

   _____

   _____

9. What are plate boundaries?

   _____

   _____

10. Why is it good that newer buildings sway in an earthquake?

   _____

   _____

All about Earthquakes (continued)

Grammar, Usage, and Mechanics

Read each item. Fill in the correct answer.

1. Which word is an adjective that describes the wind?

   A _____ wind can be dangerous.

   (A) toward
   (B) shift
   (C) energy
   (D) strong

2. In which sentence is the adjective underlined?

   (A) The yellow <u>butterfly</u> flew carefully to the flower.
   (B) The <u>yellow</u> butterfly flew carefully to the flower.
   (C) The yellow butterfly flew <u>carefully</u> to the flower.
   (D) The yellow butterfly <u>flew</u> carefully to the flower.

3. How are adjectives most often used?

   (A) to describe nouns using sensory details
   (B) to describe an adjective
   (C) to modify an action or linking verb
   (D) to indicate the noun to which a pronoun refers

4. In which sentence are only adjectives underlined?

   (A) The deep <u>canyon</u> was <u>formed</u> by an ancient earthquake.
   (B) The deep canyon was formed by an <u>ancient</u> <u>earthquake</u>.
   (C) The <u>deep</u> canyon was formed by an <u>ancient</u> earthquake.
   (D) The deep <u>canyon</u> was formed by an <u>ancient</u> earthquake.

5. Which adjective would describe the shape of an object?

   (A) colorful
   (B) slowly
   (C) round
   (D) mysterious

All about Earthquakes (continued)
Analyzing the Selection

Read the question below. Write complete sentences for your answer. Support your answer with evidence from the selection.

What are some things that are caused by earthquakes?

_____

_____

_____

_____

_____

_____

_____

_____

_____

_____

_____

_____

_____

_____

_____

_____

_____

_____

_____

_____

Name _____ **Date** _____

People have learned how to live with earthquakes.	1-8
We now make buildings that are safer than they	9-17
were before. None of them are perfectly safe. But	18-26
they are better than in the past.	27-33
Tall skyscrapers go hundreds of feet into the	34-41
air. These buildings are made safe in an odd way.	42-51
They are built on a special foundation. This is the	52-61
part of the building that is way under the ground.	62-71
When there is an earthquake, the building slides	72-79
back and forth. It moves just a little bit. It doesn't	80-90
fall over. The people inside are safe.	91-97
Many buildings are made of concrete. We can	98-105
make the concrete stronger. There are steel rods	106-113
in the concrete. This happens when the concrete	114-121
is still soft. The rods keep the building from	122-130
collapsing during an earthquake. If the concrete	131-137
cracks, the rods will help to hold the building	138-146
together.	147
In some parts of the world, people make their	148-156
houses out of very light natural materials. When an	157-165
earthquake hits, the houses shake. They usually	166-172
don't fall. If they do, the houses are easy to fix.	173-183

Evaluating Codes for Oral Fluency

sky	(/) words read incorrectly
blue ^ sky	(^) Inserted word (]) after the last word

Reading Rate and Accuracy

Total Words Read	
Number of Errors	
Number of Correct Words Read per Minute (WCPM)	
Accuracy Rate	
(Number of Correct Words Read per Minute ÷ Total Words Read)	

Reading Prosody

	LOW	AVG.	HIGH
Decoding Ability	○	○	○
Pace	○	○	○
Syntax	○	○	○
Self-correction	○	○	○
Intonation	○	○	○

Oral Fluency Passage Information

Lexile Measure	480L
Mean Sentence Length	8.32
Mean Log Word Frequency	3.68
Word Count	183

Phonics: /ē/ spelled ee, ea, e

Read the words in the box. Choose the correct word to complete each sentence. Write the word on the line.

deep	knee	read	east	equal

1. There is an _____ number of pencils.

2. I hurt my _____ playing soccer.

3. The post office is located _____ of the bank.

4. Joe likes to _____ every night before going to bed.

5. Be careful! The water is _____.

Word Analysis: Homographs and Homophones

Read each sentence. Fill in the bubble for the correct answer.

6. Juan put a <u>bow</u> on the gift for his mom.

   In this sentence, the word <u>bow</u> sounds most like:

   cow   two   show
   ○   ○   ○

7. The <u>dove</u> flew over the garden.

   In this sentence, the word <u>dove</u> sounds most like:

   glove   drove   move
   ○   ○   ○

Fill in the bubble under the word that fits best in each sentence.

8. Her coat is over _____.
   their   there
   ○   ○

9. The worker cut the _____ with a saw.
   board   bored
   ○   ○

10. Pat _____ how to ride a horse.
    nose   knows
    ○   ○

In My Own Backyard

Vocabulary

Read each item. Fill in the correct answer.

1. What does the word *plowed* mean in this sentence?
   The farmer *plowed* the field using a big tractor.
   - Ⓐ spread seeds
   - Ⓑ removed bad weeds
   - Ⓒ turned over soil
   - Ⓓ made a fence

2. What is a synonym for *brook* in this sentence?
   The *brook* wandered through the forest.
   - Ⓐ bear
   - Ⓑ trail
   - Ⓒ turkey
   - Ⓓ stream

3. What does the word *grazed* mean in this sentence?
   The cows *grazed* in the field.
   - Ⓐ harvested
   - Ⓑ ate grass
   - Ⓒ crouched
   - Ⓓ joined a herd

4. What does the word *settlers* most likely mean in this sentence?
   It took the *settlers* months to reach the big river.
   - Ⓐ pioneers
   - Ⓑ students
   - Ⓒ tourists
   - Ⓓ herd

5. What does the word *blurry* mean in this sentence?
   My eyes feel *blurry* when I am very tired.
   - Ⓐ tired
   - Ⓑ burning
   - Ⓒ unclear
   - Ⓓ finished

In My Own Backyard (continued)

Comprehension

**Read the following items carefully and fill in the correct answer.
You may look back at the selection to answer the questions.**

1. The following question has two parts. First, answer **Part A.**
Then, answer **Part B.**

   Part A What is happening in the mind of the writer of the story?
   - (A) The writer is listening to someone's story.
   - (B) The writer is having a nightmare.
   - (C) The writer is thinking about a book.
   - (D) The writer is traveling back in time.

   Part B Which sentence from the story **best** supports your
   answer for **Part A**?
   - (A) Her voice pulled me out of the past and into the present.
   - (B) A volcano belched smoke in the distance.
   - (C) Around the coral and seaweed, unusual fish wore hard shells.
   - (D) Then all at once, right before my eyes, the sawmill
     disappeared.

2. How do you know this story is told from the first person point
   of view?
   - (A) The writer talks about men and women in the story.
   - (B) The writer explains what the settlers were doing.
   - (C) The writer uses the words "I" and "my" in the story.
   - (D) The writer had never seen animals like this before.

3. How are the sequence of events in the story organized?
   - (A) The sequence of events move through one day.
   - (B) The sequence of events move backward through time.
   - (C) The sequence of events are in the present time.
   - (D) The sequence of events are in the future.

Comprehension

4. What did the dinosaurs eat in the story?
Ⓐ palms and ferns   Ⓒ fantastic birds
Ⓑ giant dragonflies   Ⓓ lizards and centipedes

5. What time period did the writer describe first?
Ⓐ the period of the Native Americans
Ⓑ the time of the cave people
Ⓒ about a hundred years ago
Ⓓ when the settlers came through

Read the following items carefully. Use complete sentences to answer the questions.

6. What was the backyard like at the last time the writer imagined?

_____

7. What were the people like who were afraid of the big, furry elephant?

_____

8. Describe the group that came just before the settlers from Europe.

_____

9. What is a sawmill in the story?

_____

10. What time of day is the story happening, and how do you know this?

_____

_____

     Comprehension • *Assessment 1*

In My Own Backyard (continued)
Grammar, Usage, and Mechanics

1. Which answer is the correct plural form of *sport*?
   - Ⓐ sportes
   - Ⓑ sports
   - Ⓒ sporties
   - Ⓓ sport

2. Which answer is the correct plural form of *couch*?
   - Ⓐ couches
   - Ⓑ couchs
   - Ⓒ couchies
   - Ⓓ coucies

3. Which answer is the correct plural form of *fish*?
   - Ⓐ fishs
   - Ⓑ fishes
   - Ⓒ fish
   - Ⓓ fishies

4. Which answer is the correct plural form of *knife*?
   - Ⓐ knifs
   - Ⓑ knives
   - Ⓒ kinifes
   - Ⓓ knifies

5. Which answer is the correct plural form of *goose*?
   - Ⓐ goosives
   - Ⓑ gooses
   - Ⓒ geese
   - Ⓓ goosies

In My Own Backyard (continued)

Analyzing the Selection

Read the question below. Write complete sentences for your answer. Support your answer with evidence from the selection.

In your own words, describe the different ways people were living in the story.

_____

_____

_____

_____

_____

_____

_____

_____

_____

_____

_____

_____

_____

_____

_____

_____

_____

_____

_____

_____

Analyzing the Selection • *Assessment 1*

Teacher Directions: Duplicate this page for each student you choose to assess. Make one copy of the Unit 2 Lesson 5 Oral Fluency Assessment found on page 228 for students to read from.

Wayne and his friend, Jess, were playing in the park. Wayne saw a strange rock. He picked it up. It was black and shiny. He brought the rock home to show to his father.

"That's coal," Dad said. Then he asked, "Would you like to learn more about it? You might be surprised to learn how coal was mined and used here."

The next day, Dad took Wayne and Jess to a museum. It was filled with information about coal. One display case showed how coal was formed. It comes from swamps. Dead plants rotted in the swamps. Slowly, the rotting plants and other matter turned to coal.

People used to use coal to heat their homes. It is still used to make electricity and for other things. People are also trying to find ways to use coal that are safer for the environment.

As they left, Wayne's father said, "So how did you like our trip?"

"It was great," Wayne said. "I had no idea how important coal was and where it came from. It's hard to believe that where we live now was once a swamp surrounded by forests."

Line numbers
1-9
10-19
20-29
30-34
35-42
43-51
52-60
61-62
63-72
73-80
81-88
89-96
97-104
105-108
109-119
120-128
129-139
140-144
145-153
154-157
158-167
168-176
177-187
188-191

Evaluating Codes for Oral Fluency	
sky	(/) words read incorrectly
blue ^ sky	(^) Inserted word (]) after the last word

Reading Rate and Accuracy	
Total Words Read	
Number of Errors	
Number of Correct Words Read per Minute (WCPM)	
Accuracy Rate	
(Number of Correct Words Read per Minute ÷ Total Words Read)	

Reading Prosody	LOW	AVG.	HIGH
Decoding Ability	○	○	○
Pace	○	○	○
Syntax	○	○	○
Self-correction	○	○	○
Intonation	○	○	○

Oral Fluency Passage Information	
Lexile Measure	510L
Mean Sentence Length	9.14
Mean Log Word Frequency	3.78
Word Count	191

Volcano Rising

Vocabulary

Read each item. Fill in the correct answer.

1. What is a synonym for *catastrophe* in this sentence?
   Good planning helped to avoid a *catastrophe*.
   - Ⓐ tightening
   - Ⓑ ceremony
   - Ⓒ scramble
   - Ⓓ disaster

2. What does the word *seep* mean in this sentence?
   The rainwater began to *seep* across the road.
   - Ⓐ mold
   - Ⓑ spread slowly
   - Ⓒ weigh down
   - Ⓓ cover

3. What does the word *magma* most likely mean in this sentence?
   Magma moved down the side of the volcano.
   - Ⓐ melted rock
   - Ⓑ icy slush
   - Ⓒ lots of bugs
   - Ⓓ water and mud

4. What does the word *majestic* mean in this sentence?
   A *majestic* tree was at the edge of the lake.
   - Ⓐ splendid
   - Ⓑ leafy
   - Ⓒ frozen
   - Ⓓ lonesome

5. What is a synonym for *destructive* in this sentence?
   A *destructive* forest fire happened last year.
   - Ⓐ natural
   - Ⓑ gleaming
   - Ⓒ damaging
   - Ⓓ mysterious

Volcano Rising (continued)

Comprehension

Read the following items carefully and fill in the correct answer. You may look back at the selection to answer the questions.

1. The following question has two parts. First, answer **Part A**. Then, answer **Part B**.

Part A Which of these statements about volcanoes is true?
- Ⓐ Their eruptions are creative.
- Ⓑ Their eruptions are destructive.
- Ⓒ Their eruptions are both creative and destructive.
- Ⓓ Their eruptions are most likely to create mountains.

Part B Which sentence from the article **best** supports your answer for **Part A**?
- Ⓐ Volcanoes even make mountains underwater.
- Ⓑ But even gentle lava flows are hard to halt.
- Ⓒ A creative eruption can start with the ground swelling a tiny bit each year.
- Ⓓ Most volcanoes have both destructive and creative eruptions.

2. Which adjective best describes the smell of lava?
- Ⓐ stinky　　　Ⓑ gooey　　　Ⓒ sweet　　　Ⓓ hot

3. How does magma move from deep within earth to the surface?
- Ⓐ It bubbles up to a river or stream and then flows out.
- Ⓑ It rises in a tube to an opening in the surface.
- Ⓒ It forms a mountain and then seeps out the bottom.
- Ⓓ It becomes a gas and floats into the air before cooling off.

Volcano Rising (continued)
Comprehension

4. Where does the selection say a volcano might secretly erupt?

   Ⓐ within a swamp   Ⓒ under a glacier

   Ⓑ beneath a city   Ⓓ inside a cave

5. What is the most dangerous volcano called in the selection?

   Ⓐ super volcano   Ⓒ scarred land

   Ⓑ gigantic eruption   Ⓓ dome volcano

Read the following items carefully. Use complete sentences to answer the questions.

6. What are magma and lava?

_____

_____

7. What is the first sign that a volcano is going to appear?

_____

_____

8. What happens when lava hits the ocean?

_____

_____

9. Can creative eruptions be stopped?

_____

_____

10. Do people ever get close to volcano eruptions?

_____

_____

Volcano Rising (continued)

Analyzing the Selection

Read the question below. Write complete sentences for your answer. Support your answer with evidence from the selection.

Explain how a volcano can be creative.

_____

_____

_____

_____

_____

_____

_____

_____

_____

_____

_____

_____

_____

_____

_____

_____

_____

_____

_____

Name _____ **Date** _____

For most people, volcanoes are a little scary. They are exploding mountains from which lava flows. Everything near the volcano is destroyed. That is true for some volcanoes. But others are a little different and much less dangerous.	1-8 9-15 16-22 23-32 33-38
An active volcano is one that is still able to explode. These are dangerous. They don't explode very often. Even so, people are very careful.	39-48 49-55 56-63
Some volcanoes are dormant. That means they can still explode, but they probably won't. If they do, it will happen only rarely.	64-70 71-79 80-85
A third kind of volcano is an extinct volcano. This is one that has stopped exploding. It will probably never explode again. Most of the time, an extinct volcano looks just like other mountains.	86-95 96-104 105-113 114-119
In New Mexico, there is a mountain called Mt. Taylor. It is an extinct volcano. Most people don't know that. All they see is a beautiful mountain. It sits in the middle of the desert. It has snow on top in the winter, and people like to use snowshoes to get to the top. In the summer, hikers from all over come to enjoy the beautiful scenery. When they get to the top, they can see for hundreds of miles all around.	120-128 129-137 138-147 148-159 160-169 170-180 181-188 189-199 200-201

Evaluating Codes for Oral Fluency

sky	(/) words read incorrectly
blue ^ sky	(^) Inserted word ([]) after the last word

Reading Rate and Accuracy

Total Words Read:	
Number of Errors:	
Number of Correct Words Read per Minute (WCPM):	
Accuracy Rate:	
(Number of Correct Words Read per Minute ÷ Total Words Read)	

Reading Prosody

	LOW	AVG.	HIGH
Decoding Ability	○	○	○
Pace	○	○	○
Syntax	○	○	○
Self-correction	○	○	○
Intonation	○	○	○

Oral Fluency Passage Information

Lexile Measure	520L
Mean Sentence Length:	8.70
Mean Log Word Frequency	3.66
Word Count	201

Phonics: /ā/ spelled *a, a_e* and /ī/ spelled *i, i_e*

Read each sentence. Choose the word that best completes the sentence.

1. Many _____ animals live in the jungle.

    a. wilde   **b.** wild   **c.** widl

2. _____ is my favorite month of the year.

    a. April   **b.** Apryl   **c.** Aiprl

3. I took a _____ of the crunchy apple.

    a. biit   **b.** bite   **c.** bitt

4. My brother runs at a fast _____.

    a. rate   **b.** rat   **c.** raat

5. Ten cents equals a _____.

    a. dim   **b.** dime   **c.** diim

Phonics: /ō/ spelled o, o_e and /ū/ spelled u, u_e

Read each sentence. Choose the word that best completes the sentence.

6. The correct answer is _____.

   a. no   **b.** kow   **c.** nough

7. I played the _____ of a king in the play.

   a. rol   **b.** role   **c.** ro

8. My dad has a good sense of _____.

   a. humor   **b.** humer   **c.** huomor

9. I watered the flowers with the garden _____.

   a. hosi   **b.** hos   **c.** hose

10. The special wall will _____ the noise.

   a. mut   **b.** mute   **c.** muet

Phonics: /ā/, /ē/, /ī/, /ō/, /ū/

Read each sentence. Choose the word that best completes the sentence.

11. The birds were _____ to fly.

    a. free   **b.** freet   **c.** frea

12. Andrea received a _____ for her extra work.

    a. banus   **b.** boneus   **c.** bonus

13. The strong _____ was made of steel.

    a. cabel   **b.** cable   **c.** coble

14. The book had an unusual _____.

    a. titl   **b.** tetle   **c.** title

15. My friends will _____ to form a team.

    a. onite   **b.** unite   **c.** uenite

Phonics: /n/ spelled *kn_, gn* and /r/ spelled *wr_*

Read each sentence. Choose the word that best completes the sentence.

16. I _____ down to tie my shoe.

    a. knolt   **b.** knelt   **c.** nelt

17. The _____ was tiny but made a lot of noise.

    a. natt   **b.** gat   **c.** gnat

18. Fred will _____ a letter to his grandparents.

    a. write   **b.** rit   **c.** rite

19. Ned _____ he will do well on the test.

    a. knows   **b.** nose   **c.** nos

20. We decided to keep the art _____ simple.

    a. dsign   **b.** design   **c.** desgn

Name _____ **Date** _____ **Score** _____

Vocabulary

Read each item. Fill in the correct answer.

1. What is a synonym for *flows* in this sentence?
   The magma *flows* quickly down the volcano.
   Ⓐ harden
   Ⓑ streams
   Ⓒ forms
   Ⓓ gently

2. What is a synonym for *boundaries* in this sentence?
   The *boundaries* of the state were clearly marked.
   Ⓐ sirens
   Ⓑ twinkles
   Ⓒ crumbles
   Ⓓ borders

3. What does the word *secures* most likely mean in this sentence?
   A trucker *secures* the load before driving off.
   Ⓐ keeps from moving
   Ⓑ gets paid for
   Ⓒ tries to weigh
   Ⓓ adds fuel

4. What does the word *interact* mean in this sentence?
   The settlers wanted to *interact* with the people who lived in the area.
   Ⓐ learn how to keep away from
   Ⓑ sell food and water to
   Ⓒ work together with
   Ⓓ discover other areas

5. What does the word *valley* mean in this sentence?
   A sloped trail led down into the *valley*.
   Ⓐ a grassy field
   Ⓑ a sharp peak
   Ⓒ a prairie
   Ⓓ a low area between hills

Vocabulary

6. What is a synonym for *plucking* in this sentence?
The children enjoyed *plucking* berries from the bushes.
- Ⓐ picking
- Ⓑ eating
- Ⓒ liking
- Ⓓ buying

7. What does the word *tufts* most likely mean in this sentence?
Tufts of tall grass grew around the pond.
- Ⓐ acres
- Ⓑ clumps
- Ⓒ baskets
- Ⓓ weeds

8. What does the word *witness* mean in this sentence?
A few people were able to *witness* the volcano erupting.
- Ⓐ like
- Ⓑ measure
- Ⓒ force
- Ⓓ see

9. What is a synonym for *haze* in this sentence?
A light *haze* made it hard to see that morning.
- Ⓐ noise
- Ⓑ screen
- Ⓒ mist
- Ⓓ glass

10. What does the word *creative* mean in this sentence?
Jayden's teacher said his poem was very *creative*.
- Ⓐ funny
- Ⓑ boring
- Ⓒ hard to understand
- Ⓓ new and different

Comprehension: Cold Read

Read the selection. Then answer the questions.

Lena couldn't wait. She and her family were on their way to California for vacation. They had rented a house near the beach. She had never seen the ocean before. She was really excited.

"Do you kids want to see the beach first or the house?" asked Mom. She was driving, but she already knew the answer.

"The beach," all the kids said together. Dad answered the same thing.

While Mom drove, Dad looked at the map. He gave directions and told everybody about the spot they were going to.

"There are two kinds of beaches here, rocky and sandy," read Dad. "It looks like the next exit will take us to a parking area beside the beach."

Mom turned off the highway onto a smaller road. In just a few minutes, they saw signs for the parking area. Mom drove carefully and followed the signs. Then they saw it, the ocean.

No one said a word. Mom stopped the car. They all just looked. Then they all started to talk at once except Mom. She found a parking spot. As soon as she stopped, the doors flew open and everybody jumped out.

The parking lot was in a small area on top of a cliff. The cliff was about a hundred feet above the ocean. There was a stairway that led from the parking area down to the beach. On the right, the shoreline was steep and rocky. On the left, it was flat and sandy.

"This is even better than I thought," sighed Lena. "The ocean just seems to go on forever."

"Can we go down to the beach?" asked her brother, Norman. He was already standing at the top of the stairs.

"Okay, but wait for the rest of us," said Mom.

They all went down the steps carefully. They were steep, but another reason to go slowly was to look at the rocky cliff. It was beautiful. There were plants growing out of some places in the rocks.

The steps went down to the sandy beach at the base of the cliff. They all took off their shoes and ran into the water up to their knees. The waves moved in and out. Lena felt the sand moving around her toes.

"Why don't the waves move all the sand away?" asked Lena.

Mom answered, "Most of the time, the waves move the sand back and forth. If there is a big storm, the waves might move the sand to a different place."

While they were talking, Norman had walked back to the beach. He put his sandals on and dashed over to where the sand ended and the rocky part of the beach began. He walked out on some rocks and stared into a pool of water.

"Wow, look at this!" he shouted and pointed into the water. He was so excited that he almost fell in.

They walked over to where Norman was standing. There was a pool of water among the rocks. In the pool were some fish, shellfish, crabs, seaweed, and something that looked like a flower. They were amazed at how beautiful the pool was, and they knew that this was going to be the best vacation ever.

Comprehension: Cold Read • *Assessment 1*

Comprehension

Read the following items carefully and answer the questions.

1. What was the beach like near the parking area?
   - Ⓐ It had pools in the rocks with fish and seaweed.
   - Ⓑ Rocky on one side and sandy on the other.
   - Ⓒ A cliff went right down to the water.
   - Ⓓ Flat and smooth like a parking area.

2. What inference can you make from Mom's question, "Do you kids want to see the beach first or the house?"
   - Ⓐ The house was really far away from where they were.
   - Ⓑ They had seen the house already on another visit.
   - Ⓒ They were more interested in the beach than the house.
   - Ⓓ The house was right beside the beach near the parking area.

3. What might happen to the sand if there is a big storm?
   - Ⓐ the waves will help plants grow out of it
   - Ⓑ the waves might move the sand to a different place
   - Ⓒ the sand becomes a pool of water
   - Ⓓ the sand becomes a rocky beach

4. How were the two types of beaches different?
   - Ⓐ The rocky part had more living things than the sandy part.
   - Ⓑ You had to go down steps to get to the sandy part.
   - Ⓒ The sandy part had waves and the rocky part did not.
   - Ⓓ You could only see the sandy part from the car.

5. What was the main cause for the family to walk slowly down the steps?
   - Ⓐ the slippery steps
   - Ⓑ looking at the rocky cliff
   - Ⓒ wind blowing sand
   - Ⓓ the water up to their knees

Grammar, Usage, and Mechanics

Read each item. Fill in the correct answer.

1. Choose the answer that is a complete sentence.
Ⓐ The tall bird stood in the shallow water.
Ⓑ Running along the bank of the river.
Ⓒ The small pond home to frogs and turtles.
Ⓓ Fish because the river not frozen in winter.

2. Which of these sentences is declarative?
Ⓐ Open the box near the window carefully.
Ⓑ How old do you think the clock in the attic is?
Ⓒ Be careful moving that old clock!
Ⓓ The old clock was in the family's attic.

3. Which of these sentences is interrogative?
Ⓐ Get out of that tree before you fall!
Ⓑ Did anyone see where the cat got to?
Ⓒ Put some food in the dish for the cat.
Ⓓ The cat is asleep on the arm of the couch.

4. Which of these sentences is exclamatory?
Ⓐ The rain stopped around midnight.
Ⓑ Whose idea was it to go for a hike?
Ⓒ Yikes, this mud is really sticky!
Ⓓ Take your shoes off before coming inside.

5. Which of these sentences is imperative?
Ⓐ Get some ice out of the freezer.
Ⓑ How did you hurt your foot?
Ⓒ This trail is really rocky.
Ⓓ Don't slip on that wet rock!

Grammar, Usage, and Mechanics

6. Which sentence has correct punctuation?
- Ⓐ Wasn't that watermelon delicious
- Ⓑ Wasn't that watermelon delicious?
- Ⓒ Wasn't that watermelon delicious.
- Ⓓ Wasn't that watermelon delicious!

7. Which sentence has correct capitalization?
- Ⓐ The streets in boston were covered with Snow.
- Ⓑ The Streets in Boston were covered with snow.
- Ⓒ The streets in boston were covered with snow.
- Ⓓ The streets in Boston were covered with snow.

8. In which sentence is an adjective underlined?
- Ⓐ At one end of the valley was a <u>shallow</u> pond.
- Ⓑ At one end of the <u>valley</u> was a shallow pond.
- Ⓒ At one <u>end</u> of the valley was a shallow pond.
- Ⓓ At one end of the valley was a shallow <u>pond</u>.

9. Which answer is the correct plural form of *child*?
- Ⓐ child
- Ⓑ childies
- Ⓒ children
- Ⓓ childs

10. Which answer is the correct plural form of *tooth*?
- Ⓐ tooth
- Ⓑ tooths
- Ⓒ toothes
- Ⓓ teeth

Spelling

Choose the correct way to spell the underlined word. If the underlined word is correct, choose the last answer, *Leave as is*. Fill in the correct answer.

1. The weather is <u>mield</u> for this time of year.
   Ⓐ miled
   Ⓑ mild
   Ⓒ meild
   Ⓓ Leave as is.

2. Here is today's <u>paper</u>.
   Ⓐ papr
   Ⓑ peaper
   Ⓒ paaper
   Ⓓ Leave as is.

3. We finished the first <u>uunit</u> of the book.
   Ⓐ uenit
   Ⓑ uneit
   Ⓒ unit
   Ⓓ Leave as is.

4. Grass covered <u>moost</u> of the lawn.
   Ⓐ most
   Ⓑ moast
   Ⓒ moest
   Ⓓ Leave as is.

5. Did you <u>rite</u> a new story?
   Ⓐ rwite
   Ⓑ wite
   Ⓒ write
   Ⓓ Leave as is.

Spelling

6. What does that <u>sine</u> say?
- Ⓐ sinne
- Ⓑ sign
- Ⓒ sain
- Ⓓ Leave as is.

7. The officer <u>spoak</u> to our class.
- Ⓐ spoke
- Ⓑ spok
- Ⓒ spoek
- Ⓓ Leave as is.

8. Let's <u>begin</u> with a warm-up.
- Ⓐ beegin
- Ⓑ bgin
- Ⓒ beagin
- Ⓓ Leave as is.

9. What time did you go to <u>sleap</u>?
- Ⓐ slepe
- Ⓑ slep
- Ⓒ sleep
- Ⓓ Leave as is.

10. The boards <u>creke</u> when we walk on them.
- Ⓐ crek
- Ⓑ creak
- Ⓒ criek
- Ⓓ Leave as is.

Teacher Directions: Duplicate this page for each student you choose to assess. Make one copy of the
Unit 2 Oral Fluency Assessment found on page 230 for students to read from.

Earth changes in many ways. Some are small,	1-8
and you don't see them. Others are large. Different	9-17
things cause these changes.	18-21
One thing that causes changes is water. Think	22-29
about a rain storm. Some of the water flows	30-38
quickly down hills. It goes fast if the hills are	39-48
steep, and the flowing water moves dirt and rocks.	49-57
When this happens, deep cuts can be formed. One	58-66
type of cut is called a valley. Another is a canyon.	67-77
Moving water made one of our country's most	78-85
famous sights. It's the Grand Canyon, and it is	86-94
more than a mile deep.	95-99
Wind can also change things on Earth. Sand	100-107
can be found on a beach or in the desert. When	108-118
the wind blows, the sand moves around. It forms	119-127
hills called dunes. Sometimes these hills can be	128-135
hundreds of feet high.	136-139

Evaluating Codes for Oral Fluency

sky	(/) words read incorrectly
blue ^ sky	(^) Inserted word ([]) after the last word

Reading Rate and Accuracy

Total Words Read	
Number of Errors	
Number of Correct Words Read per Minute (WCPM)	
Accuracy Rate	
(Number of Correct Words Read per Minute ÷ Total Words Read)	

Reading Prosody

	LOW	AVG.	HIGH
Decoding Ability	○	○	○
Pace	○	○	○
Syntax	○	○	○
Self-correction	○	○	○
Intonation	○	○	○

Oral Fluency Passage Information

Lexile Measure	450L
Mean Sentence Length	7.72
Mean Log Word Frequency	3.62
Word Count	139

Name _____ **Date** _____ **Score** _____

Informative Writing Task

Write an informative story about the place you live. Include details and descriptive language so the reader will get a good picture of the place. When you write, remember to
- express your ideas clearly.
- use correct grammar, spelling, punctuation, and capitalization.

_____

_____

_____

_____

_____

_____

_____

_____

_____

_____

_____

_____

_____

_____

_____

_____

_____

_____

Four Point Rubrics for Informative Writing

Genre	1 Point	2 Points	3 Points	4 Points
Informative Writing	Writing has no introduction or clear topic. It offers a group of loosely related facts or a series of poorly related written steps. No conclusion is included.	Writing is clearly organized around main points with supportive facts or assertions. Writing has no clear introduction, but its topic is identifiable. However, it includes many facts unrelated to the topic, or it describes things in a disorganized way. No conclusion is included.	Main points and supportive details can be identified, but they are not clearly marked. Writing has an introduction and offers facts about the topic. Some facts may be irrelevant, or some ideas may be vague or out of order. The writing is fairly well organized but does not have a strong conclusion.	Traces and constructs a line of argument, identifying part-to-whole relations. Main points are supported with logical and appropriate evidence. Writing begins with an introduction and offers relevant facts about the topic or describes the topic appropriately. The writing is organized using cause/effect, compare/contrast, or another pattern. It ends with a strong conclusion.

Writing Traits

	1 Point	2 Points	3 Points	4 Points
Focus	Topic is unclear or wanders and must be inferred. Extraneous material may be present.	Topic/position/direction is unclear and must be inferred.	Topic/position is stated and direction/purpose is previewed and maintained. Mainly stays on topic.	Topic/position is clearly stated, previewed, and maintained throughout the paper. Topics and details are tied together with a central theme or purpose that is maintained/threaded throughout the paper.
Ideas/Content	Superficial and/or minimal content is included.	Main ideas are understandable, although they may be overly broad or simplistic, and the results may not be effective. Supporting detail is limited, insubstantial, overly general, or off topic.	The writing is clear and focused. The reader can easily understand the main ideas. Support is present, although it may be limited or rather general.	Writing is exceptionally clear, focused, and interesting. Main ideas stand out and are developed by strong support and rich details.
Elaboration (supporting details and examples that develop the main idea)	States ideas or points with minimal detail to support them.	Includes sketchy, redundant, or general details; some may be irrelevant. Support for key ideas is very uneven.	Includes mix of general statements and specific details/examples. Support is mostly relevant but may be uneven and lack depth in places.	Includes specific details and relevant supporting examples for each key point/idea.

Writing Conventions

	1 Point	2 Points	3 Points	4 Points
Conventions Overall	Numerous errors in usage, grammar, spelling, capitalization, and punctuation repeatedly distract the reader and make the text difficult to read. The reader finds it difficult to focus on the message.	The writing demonstrates limited control of standard writing conventions (punctuation, spelling, grammar, and usage). Errors sometimes impede readability.	The writing demonstrates control of standard writing conventions (punctuation, spelling, grammar, and usage). Minor errors, while perhaps noticeable, do not impede readability.	The writing demonstrates exceptionally strong control of standard writing conventions (punctuation, spelling, grammar, and usage) and uses them effectively to enhance communication. Errors are so few and so minor that the reader can easily skim over them.

Phonics: /ā/ spelled *ai_*, *_ay*

Unscramble the following words. Write the word on the line, and write *ai_* or *_ay* to tell the spelling pattern.

1. y t a s   _____   _____

2. d i a p   _____   _____

3. t y a r   _____   _____

4. a l i d   _____   _____

5. l y a p   _____   _____

Phonics: /ā/ spelled a, a_e

April trace late flavor bale

Choose a word from the box above to complete each sentence. Write the word on the line.

6. Follow the line to _____ the pattern.

7. My favorite _____ of ice cream is cherry.

8. It often rains in the month of _____.

9. I cannot be _____ for swim practice.

10. The farmer lifted the _____ of hay.

Gross Jobs

Vocabulary

Read each item. Fill in the correct answer.

1. What is a synonym for *ensure* in this sentence?
The builder will *ensure* that the door is working.
Ⓐ appreciate
Ⓑ clutch
Ⓒ dismiss
Ⓓ guarantee

2. What does the word *flee* most likely mean in this sentence?
People had to *flee* the rising water.
Ⓐ go swimming in
Ⓑ look for
Ⓒ run away from
Ⓓ get dressed

3. What does the word *flexible* mean in this sentence?
The rubber hose was strong and *flexible*.
Ⓐ able to be bent
Ⓑ easily hurt
Ⓒ longer
Ⓓ kind

4. What is a synonym for *vital* in this sentence?
The plane brought *vital* supplies to the people.
Ⓐ delicious
Ⓑ important
Ⓒ expensive
Ⓓ packaged

5. What does the word *install* mean in this sentence?
The workers will *install* a new heater.
Ⓐ buy on sale
Ⓑ try to fix
Ⓒ look at carefully
Ⓓ put in place

Gross Jobs (continued)

Comprehension

Read the following items carefully and fill in the correct answer. You may look back at the selection to answer the questions.

1. The following question has two parts. First, answer **Part A**. Then, answer **Part B**.

   Part A Why is it important that trash gets picked up often?
   Ⓐ It is put in a bag.   Ⓒ It can get stinky.
   Ⓑ It can get wet.   Ⓓ It is hard to walk around.

   Part B Which sentence from the article **best** supports your answer for **Part A**?
   Ⓐ Garbage collectors are one part of an entire team of workers who handle trash.
   Ⓑ That allows the pipe to become unblocked.
   Ⓒ As we acquire these things, we create waste.
   Ⓓ Trash that sits outside in a garbage can all week can get very stinky.

2. Why did the author write this article?
   Ⓐ to inform the reader about important jobs
   Ⓑ to express an opinion about school custodians
   Ⓒ to persuade the reader that many jobs are messy
   Ⓓ to entertain the reader with funny work stories

3. Why do insects go into buildings?
   Ⓐ to make people itch   Ⓒ to find food and shelter
   Ⓑ to look for other insects   Ⓓ to avoid garbage trucks

Gross Jobs (continued)

Comprehension

4. Which phrase from the article describes all the jobs?
- Ⓐ pest control
- Ⓑ dirty work
- Ⓒ waste water
- Ⓓ entire team

5. What is the greatest danger of clogged pipes?
- Ⓐ You can't cook or wash the dishes.
- Ⓑ The shower doesn't work right.
- Ⓒ Waste water cannot exit the home.
- Ⓓ It takes too long to water the garden.

Read the following items carefully. Answer the questions.

6. Beside each heading, summarize what that part of the article is all about.

Pipe Problems _____

What's That Smell? _____

The Clean Team _____

Creepy Critter Control _____

7. What is the snake in the article?

_____

8. How do you know that using poison to control insects is dangerous?

_____

9. Why do workers at a landfill cover garbage with soil?

_____

10. Why are the names of the workers in bold print in the article?

_____

Gross Jobs (continued)

Grammar, Usage, and Mechanics

Read each item. Fill in the correct answer.

1. Which of these sentences has correct punctuation?
- Ⓐ This is my house, said Sandy.
- Ⓑ "This is my house, said Sandy.
- Ⓒ "This is my house," said Sandy.
- Ⓓ This is my house," said Sandy.

2. Which of these sentences has correct punctuation?
- Ⓐ "How can we help?" asked Ruben.
- Ⓑ How can we help? asked Ruben.
- Ⓒ "How can we help? asked Ruben.
- Ⓓ "How can we help? asked Ruben."

3. Which of these sentences has correct punctuation?
- Ⓐ "Ms. Ryan said, We are going to the nature center."
- Ⓑ Ms. Ryan said, "We are going to the nature center.
- Ⓒ Ms. Ryan said "We are going to the nature center."
- Ⓓ Ms. Ryan said, "We are going to the nature center."

4. Which of these sentences has correct punctuation?
- Ⓐ Mr. Hill asked "Would you like some juice?"
- Ⓑ Mr. Hill asked, "Would you like some juice?"
- Ⓒ Mr. Hill asked, "Would you like some juice?
- Ⓓ Mr. Hill asked, Would you like some juice?

5. Which of these sentences has correct punctuation?
- Ⓐ Hand me the wrench, said the plumber.
- Ⓑ "Hand me the wrench" said the plumber.
- Ⓒ "Hand me the wrench," said the plumber.
- Ⓐ "Hand me the wrench, said the plumber."

Gross Jobs (continued)

Analyzing the Selection

Read the question below. Write complete sentences for your answer. Support your answer with evidence from the selection.

Why are the jobs described in the article so important?

_____

_____

_____

_____

_____

_____

_____

_____

_____

_____

_____

_____

_____

_____

_____

_____

_____

Teacher Directions: Duplicate this page for each student you choose to assess. Make one copy of the Unit 3 Lesson 1 Oral Fluency Assessment found on page 231 for students to read from.

There was a knock at the door. | 1-7

"Can you get that?" Mom said. She was with | 8-16
the baby. | 17-18

Brian opened the door, and saw that his neighbor, | 19-27
Mr. Green, was there. | 28-31

"Hi, Mr. Green," Brian said. | 32-36

"Brian, you're just the person I wanted to talk | 37-45
to," Mr. Green said. He explained that he had to go | 46-56
out of town and needed someone to feed his pets | 57-66
while he was gone. He asked Brian to do it. | 67-76

"No problem," Brian said. "I like animals, and | 77-84
I would really enjoy it." | 85-89

The next day Brian went to Mr. Green's house. | 90-98
First he fed the fish. Brian liked all their bright | 99-108
colors. He laughed when they raced to catch the | 109-117
fish food as it floated on the water. | 118-125

Next Brian put food and water in the cat's dish. | 126-135
Daisy the cat was curled up on the sofa. Brian | 136-145
played with Daisy, who loved to chase a colorful | 146-154
ball. Then he petted her. Daisy purred loudly. | 155-162

"This is a great job," Brian thought. "I hope I can | 163-173
do it every week." | 174-177

Evaluating Codes for Oral Fluency

sky	(/) words read incorrectly
blue ^ sky	(^) Inserted word ([) after the last word

Reading Rate and Accuracy

Total Words Read	
Number of Errors	
Number of Correct Words Read per Minute (WCPM)	
Accuracy Rate	
(Number of Correct Words Read per Minute ÷ Total Words Read)	

Reading Prosody

	LOW	AVG.	HIGH
Decoding Ability	○	○	○
Pace	○	○	○
Syntax	○	○	○
Self-correction	○	○	○
Intonation	○	○	○

Oral Fluency Passage Information

Lexile Measure	430L
Mean Sentence Length	8.43
Mean Log Word Frequency	3.83
Word Count	177

Phonics: /ē/ spelled _ie, _y, _ey

Fill in the bubble under the correct spelling of each word.

1. feeld   field   felde
   ○   ○   ○

2. chief   cheif   cheef
   ○   ○   ○

3. babi   babey   baby
   ○   ○   ○

4. penny   penni   penniy
   ○   ○   ○

5. donky   donkey   donkee
   ○   ○   ○

Phonics: /ē/ spelled ee, ea, e, e_e

**Choose the word that completes each sentence.
Write the word on the line.**

6. The king and _____ ruled the land.

   (queen, quean)

7. The squirrel lay _____ the bush.

   (underneath, underneeth)

8. The sound of the bird's soft _____ woke me up.

   (tweet, tweat)

9. The balloon was filled with _____ .

   (heelium, helium)

10. The _____ road has no bumps.

   (even, eaven)

My Community and Me
Vocabulary

Read each item. Fill in the correct answer.

1. What does the word *develop* mean in this sentence?
The inventor wants to *develop* a new kind of pen.
   - Ⓐ show to people
   - Ⓑ write a story with
   - Ⓒ sell to others
   - Ⓓ bring into being

2. What is a synonym for *polite* in this sentence?
The visitors were very *polite* to everyone.
   - Ⓐ courteous
   - Ⓑ expressive
   - Ⓒ generous
   - Ⓓ talkative

3. What does the word *relies* most likely mean in this sentence?
The town *relies* on a deep well for water.
   - Ⓐ succeeds
   - Ⓑ hitches
   - Ⓒ depends
   - Ⓓ rumbles

4. What does the word *role* mean in this sentence?
Are you going to try out for a *role* in the play?
   - Ⓐ a scene
   - Ⓑ a part played by a person
   - Ⓒ an explanation
   - Ⓓ a surprise

5. What is a synonym for *discover* in this sentence?
People *discover* new things almost every day.
   - Ⓐ discuss
   - Ⓑ clean
   - Ⓒ find
   - Ⓓ drive

My Community and Me (continued)
Comprehension

Read the following items carefully and fill in the correct answer. You may look back at the selection to answer the questions.

1. The following question has two parts. First, answer **Part A**. Then, answer **Part B**.

   Part A Which answer **best** describes roles and responsibilities?
   Ⓐ At school you are about the same as at home.
   Ⓑ Neighbors trust you.
   Ⓒ You are always the same in your family.
   Ⓓ They change over time.

   Part B Which sentence from the selection **best** supports your answer for **Part A**?
   Ⓐ As you grow older, your roles and responsibilities within your community will evolve.
   Ⓑ When you were a baby, you needed your parents for everything.
   Ⓒ One of your most important roles at school is being a student.
   Ⓓ You may give a friendly wave to the people who live next door, or you may stop to chat with them.

2. What was the author's purpose in writing this selection?
   Ⓐ to entertain the reader with funny stores about life
   Ⓑ to convince the reader that your community is an interesting place
   Ⓒ to inform the reader about different roles in life
   Ⓓ to persuade the reader to make more friends at school

My Community and Me (continued)
Comprehension

3. What is an example of friends growing apart?
   (A) They decide that they all want the same pet.
   (B) They might move or go to a different school.
   (C) They want to be good neighbors to new families.
   (D) They are true and loyal friends who know each other.

4. In the story, being a student is compared to
   (A) a job.   (B) a game.   (C) a pet.   (D) a toy.

5. A subject in school that is challenging is one that is
   (A) a hidden talent.   (C) really fascinating.
   (B) not very important.   (D) harder to learn.

Read the following items carefully. Use complete sentences to answer the questions.

6. Match the roles on the right with the places on the left.

   Family   Neighbor

   School   Classmate

   Community   Child

7. How is being a sibling different from being a son or daughter?

   _____

8. What are some family responsibilities mentioned in the story?

   _____

9. How can classmates help their peers?

   _____

10. How do neighbors change?

   _____

Name _____ **Date** _____ **Score** _____

My Community and Me (continued)
Grammar, Usage, and Mechanics

Read each item. Fill in the correct answer.

1. Choose the article that completes the sentence.
   _____ red grapes are sweeter than the green grapes.
   - Ⓐ A
   - Ⓑ The
   - Ⓒ An
   - Ⓓ Are

2. Choose the article that completes the sentence.
   Did you know that _____ elephant is larger than a giraffe?
   - Ⓐ the
   - Ⓑ a
   - Ⓒ is
   - Ⓓ an

3. Choose the article that completes the sentence.
   Tonight there will be _____ full moon.
   - Ⓐ a
   - Ⓑ the
   - Ⓒ are
   - Ⓓ an

4. In which sentence is the underlined word correct?
   - Ⓐ This goat is <u>tall</u> than that one.
   - Ⓑ This goat is <u>tallest</u> than that one.
   - Ⓒ This goat is <u>taller</u> than that one.
   - Ⓓ This goat is <u>talling</u> than that one.

5. In which sentence is the underlined word correct?
   - Ⓐ Today is the <u>warmer</u> day of the year.
   - Ⓑ Today is the <u>warmest</u> day of the year.
   - Ⓒ Today is the <u>warm</u> day of the year.
   - Ⓓ Today is the <u>warmed</u> day of the year.

My Community and Me (continued)
Analyzing the Selection

Read the question below. Write complete sentences for your answer. Support your answer with evidence from the selection.

According to the selection, how does life change as a person gets older?

_____

_____

_____

_____

_____

_____

_____

_____

_____

_____

_____

_____

_____

_____

_____

_____

Teacher Directions: Duplicate this page for each student you choose to assess. Make one copy of the Unit 3 Lesson 2 Oral Fluency Assessment found on page 232 for students to read from.

When I got to school, I was in for a surprise. My teacher said the class was going on a field trip. She said we would visit a woodcarver's shop.

A special bus took the class to the shop. The shop was nice and cozy. It had a large wood stove. Shelves along the walls were filled with carvings. Even the tables and benches in the shop were carved.

We sat down and watched one woodcarver while he worked. He showed us how to slice, whittle, and drill. He showed us how to make notches as well.

A second one did something different. She was looking at pieces of wood. She showed us how she chose wood for her carvings.

I asked if there were any of their finished pieces we could see. The first woodcarver smiled proudly. Then he pointed at a large carving of a crane. He told us it was going to a gift shop a few blocks away. I decided to visit that shop soon. I really liked the crane. It would be a perfect gift for my parents.

	1-12
	13-22
	23-30
	31-40
	41-51
	52-59
	60-68
	69
	70-77
	78-87
	88-97
	98-105
	106-115
	116-120
	121-130
	131-138
	139-149
	150-161
	162-171
	172-182
	183

Evaluating Codes for Oral Fluency

sky	(/) words read incorrectly
blue ^ sky	(^) Inserted word ([) after the last word

Reading Rate and Accuracy

Total Words Read	
Number of Errors	
Number of Correct Words Read per Minute (WCPM)	
Accuracy Rate	
(Number of Correct Words Read per Minute ÷ Total Words Read)	

Reading Prosody

	LOW	AVG.	HIGH
Decoding Ability	○	○	○
Pace	○	○	○
Syntax	○	○	○
Self-correction	○	○	○
Intonation	○	○	○

Oral Fluency Passage Information

Lexile Measure	460L
Mean Sentence Length	8.71
Mean Log Word Frequency	3.82
Word Count	183

Phonics: /ā/ spelled *a, a_e, ai_, _ay*

Read the word in the box above the question. Then read the sentence. Change the word in the box to make a new rhyming word that completes the sentence. Write the word on the line.

tail

1. The _____ boat moves with the wind.

Say

2. _____ I please go to Jack's house?

raid

3. I get _____ every week at my job.

gave

4. The computer will _____ my file.

staple

5. A huge _____ tree stands in our yard.

Phonics: /f/ spelled *ph* and /m/ spelled *_mb*

**Choose a word that best completes the sentence,
and write the word on the line.**

6. I hit my _____ with the hammer.

(thum, thumb)

7. Sue will _____ her parents at 9:00 P.M. sharp.

(phone, phon)

8. The _____ shows how Jill spends her allowance.

(graph, graf)

9. Dad will _____ the ladder to reach the roof.

(climb, clim)

10. My fingers are _____ from being in the cold weather.

(num, numb)

Phonics: Silent Letters

On the line beside the word, write the silent letter.

11. half _____

12. sword _____

13. guard _____

14. soften _____

15. column _____

Victor's Journal

Vocabulary

Read each item. Fill in the correct answer.

1. What does the word *cement* mean in this sentence?
   If you mix *cement* with water, sand, and rock it will form concrete.
   - Ⓐ a powder used in building
   - Ⓑ long pieces of wood
   - Ⓒ steel nails
   - Ⓓ a hard surface

2. What is a synonym for *blueprints* in this sentence?
   The workers looked carefully at the *blueprints*.
   - Ⓐ tools   Ⓒ plans
   - Ⓑ walls   Ⓓ routes

3. What does the word *frame* most likely mean in this sentence?
   The *frame* of the house was the first thing that the workers made.
   - Ⓐ outside roof
   - Ⓑ inside structure
   - Ⓒ basement wall
   - Ⓓ plumbing and electric

4. What does the word *insulated* mean in this sentence?
   The electric wires were *insulated* to prevent shocks.
   - Ⓐ put in a box that was completely closed
   - Ⓑ connected to an outlet in a wall
   - Ⓒ wrapped with protective covering
   - Ⓓ hung on hooks near the roof of a house

5. What is a synonym for *controller* in this sentence?
   The worker moved the *controller* on the big machine.
   - Ⓐ wheels
   - Ⓑ lever
   - Ⓒ blade
   - Ⓓ light

Victor's Journal (continued)
Comprehension

Read the following items. You may look back at the selection to answer the questions.

1. The following question has two parts. First answer **Part A**. Then answer **Part B**.

    Part A What is the journal describing?
    Ⓐ adding solar panels to a school
    Ⓑ the founding of a new town
    Ⓒ the building of a new school
    Ⓓ clearing a field down the street

    Part B Which sentence **best** supports your answer for **Part A**?
    Ⓐ Our town held a vote and decided to build a new school.
    Ⓑ Then another dump truck drove onto the field to take another load.
    Ⓒ I am looking out my bedroom window as I write this entry.
    Ⓓ My town has grown very quickly.

2. Which of these statements about the journal is true?
    Ⓐ It is written from the school's point of view.
    Ⓑ It tells about the school that the writer attends now.
    Ⓒ It describes what happened before the writer was born.
    Ⓓ It is written from the first person point of view.

3. Which of these statements is an opinion?
    Ⓐ These pipes are dug deep in the ground.
    Ⓑ The cranes are my favorite machines.
    Ⓒ The tub turns when the truck moves.
    Ⓓ There are fourteen solar panels in all.

Victor's Journal (continued)

Comprehension

4. What will be done with the vegetables from the garden?
- Ⓐ They will be eaten by players on the soccer team.
- Ⓑ They will be given to the new school's students.
- Ⓒ They will be used in the school cafeteria.
- Ⓓ They will be shared with the community.

5. How will the solar panels help the school?
- Ⓐ They look like something from a science fiction movie.
- Ⓑ They will be black and silver.
- Ⓒ They will let light into the school.
- Ⓓ They will cut the electricity bill in half.

Read the following items carefully. Answer the questions.

6. Describe the two settings for this story.

_____

7. Match the machine on the left with its function on the right.

bulldozer	lift solar panels to roof
dump truck	move dirt away from field
excavator	scrape up dirt
crane	scoop dirt out of ground

8. Why is the town building a new school?

_____

9. How does the writer describe the cranes in the journal?

_____

10. Write one fact and one opinion about the interview in the journal.

_____

Comprehension • *Assessment 1*

Victor's Journal (continued)
Grammar, Usage, and Mechanics

Read each item. Fill in the correct answer.

1. Which of these sentences has correct capitalization?
- Ⓐ The new high school will open in october.
- Ⓑ The new High School will open in October.
- Ⓒ The new high school will open in October.
- Ⓓ The new High School will open in october.

2. Which of these sentences has correct capitalization?
- Ⓐ We are going to cook Thanksgiving dinner at home.
- Ⓑ We are going to cook thanksgiving dinner at home.
- Ⓒ We are going to cook Thanksgiving Dinner at home.
- Ⓓ We are going to cook Thanksgiving dinner at Home.

3. Which of these sentences has correct capitalization?
- Ⓐ My sister is going to College in dallas.
- Ⓑ My sister is going to College in Dallas.
- Ⓒ My sister is going to college in dallas.
- Ⓓ My sister is going to college in Dallas.

4. Which of these sentences has correct capitalization?
- Ⓐ The sporting goods store is having a Sale on Saturday.
- Ⓑ The sporting goods store is having a sale on Saturday.
- Ⓒ The Sporting Goods store is having a sale on Saturday.
- Ⓓ The sporting goods store is having a sale on saturday.

5. Which of these sentences has correct capitalization?
- Ⓐ The coast of Oregon has many Beautiful Beaches.
- Ⓑ The coast of Oregon has many beautiful beaches.
- Ⓒ The coast of oregon has many beautiful beaches.
- Ⓓ The Coast of Oregon has many beautiful beaches.

Victor's Journal (continued)

Analyzing the Selection

Read the question below. Write complete sentences for your answer. Support your answer with evidence from the selection.

How does the writer mix fact and opinion in the journal?

_____

_____

_____

_____

_____

_____

_____

_____

_____

_____

_____

_____

_____

_____

_____

_____

_____

Analyzing the Selection • *Assessment 1*

Teacher Directions: Duplicate this page for each student you choose to assess. Make one copy of the Unit 3 Lesson 3 Oral Fluency Assessment found on page 233 for students to read from.

It was a rainy day, and there wasn't anything | 1-9
interesting to do. Lena's uncle thought they should | 10-17
build a kite. Lena had no idea you could build a | 18-28
kite, but she thought it was a great idea. | 29-37

Lena's uncle found some thin sticks to build the | 38-46
frame. Next, he put tissue paper over the frame. | 47-55
The paper had to be glued down. It would take time | 56-66
for the glue to dry. Lena's aunt made lunch. It was | 67-77
the perfect way to wait for the glue to dry. | 78-87

Lena found some old pieces of cloth for the kite's | 88-97
tail. She helped her uncle rip the cloth into strips. | 98-107
Then she tied the shorter strips onto a string. This | 108-117
would be the tail for the kite. | 118-124

They attached the tail to the kite. Then they | 125-133
got a ball of string. Lena's uncle tied the string to | 134-144
the kite, and he and Lena walked outside. They | 145-153
stopped and looked around. The air was still. The | 154-162
leaves on the tree were not moving. | 163-169

"We're missing one thing," said Lena's uncle. "There | 170-177
is no wind. And we can't do anything about that!" | 178-187

Evaluating Codes for Oral Fluency	
sky	(/) words read incorrectly
blue ^ sky	(^) Inserted word ([]) after the last word

Reading Rate and Accuracy	
Total Words Read	
Number of Errors	
Number of Correct Words Read per Minute (WCPM)	
Accuracy Rate	
(Number of Correct Words Read per Minute ÷ Total Words Read)	

Reading Prosody			
	LOW	AVG.	HIGH
Decoding Ability	○	○	○
Pace	○	○	○
Syntax	○	○	○
Self-correction	○	○	○
Intonation	○	○	○

Oral Fluency Passage Information	
Lexile Measure	460L
Mean Sentence Length	8.50
Mean Log Word Frequency	3.77
Word Count	187

Phonics: /s/ spelled *ce*, *ci_*, *cy*

Choose a word from the box below to complete each sentence. Write the word on the line.

icy circle celery spicy face

1. A wheel is the shape of a _____.

2. Tom made a snack tray of _____ and carrots.

3. Lois slipped on the _____ sidewalk.

4. My little brother had jelly all over his _____.

5. My mouth feels hot after eating the _____ pepper.

Phonics: /j/ spelled *ge, gi_*

Look at the pairs of words below the sentences. Choose the word that best completes the sentence. Write the word on the line.

6. The actor stepped on the _____ to read his lines.

   (stage, staje)

7. The tall man left a _____ footprint.

   (huge, huj)

8. A _____ has a long neck.

   (giraffe, geraff)

9. My best friend is the same _____ I am.

   (age, aje)

10. Mom added _____ to spice up the salad.

    (ginger, ginjer)

The Langston Times

Vocabulary

Read each item. Fill in the correct answer.

1. What does the word *blared* mean in this sentence? Music *blared* from the speakers on the stage.
- (A) convinced
- (B) made a loud sound
- (C) went around
- (D) trickled

2. What is a synonym for *movement* in this sentence?
The *movement* of the wagon train was slow but steady.
- (A) generation
- (B) labor
- (C) progress
- (D) memory

3. What does the word *value* most likely mean in this sentence?
The *value* of the coins increased over time.
- (A) worth
- (B) size
- (C) color
- (D) weight

4. What is a synonym for *result* in this sentence?
The experiment had a surprising *result*.
- (A) container
- (B) distance
- (C) expense
- (D) outcome

5. What does the word *sources* mean in this sentence?
The *sources* of the foods were easy to find.
- (A) instructions for making things
- (B) places where things came from
- (C) people who made things
- (D) ideas for the names of things

The Langston Times (continued)

Comprehension

Read the following items carefully and fill in the correct answer. You may look back at the selection to answer the questions.

1. The following question has two parts. First, answer **Part A**. Then, answer **Part B**.

   Part A Which of these words **best** describes the old school?
   Ⓐ crowded Ⓑ distant Ⓒ foolish Ⓓ disliked

   Part B Which sentence from the article **best** supports your answer for **Part A**?
   Ⓐ Langston Elementary School opens on Monday.
   Ⓑ Principal Martin Rice reported that the project went smoothly.
   Ⓒ Five years ago, town leaders decided that a new school was needed.
   Ⓓ The old school was bursting at its seams.

2. Where did this selection most likely come from?
   Ⓐ a comic book   Ⓒ a town newspaper
   Ⓑ a sports magazine   Ⓓ a picture book

3. The biggest difference between the old and new schools is
   Ⓐ location.   Ⓑ size.   Ⓒ teachers.   Ⓓ garden.

4. From the article, you can infer that the solar panels are
   Ⓐ a way to raise property values.
   Ⓑ a new source of energy.
   Ⓒ a job well done.
   Ⓓ a part of the new computer lab.

Comprehension

5. What did the sheet cover?

    Ⓐ the school's sign.   Ⓒ the school's principal.

    Ⓑ the school's band.   Ⓓ the town's mayor.

Read the following items carefully. Answer the questions.

6. Match the people in the article with what they like about the school.

Jasmine Thompson	property values will go up
Terrell Burton	solar panels
Sarah Gonzalez	community garden out back
Mayor Lopez	likes the new classrooms

7. Which caption do you like best, and why do you like it?

_____

_____

8. Why did Principal Rice like the construction company?

_____

_____

9. What does it mean to say that a neighborhood looks inviting?

_____

_____

10. How did the crowd prepare for the unveiling?

_____

_____

Name _____ Date _____ Score _____

The Langston Times (continued)

Grammar, Usage, and Mechanics

Read each item. Commas and colons have been left out of the sentences. Rewrite the sentence and put a colon and commas where they are needed.

1. The garden had tomatoes onions and peppers.

_____

_____

2. Here are today's garden volunteers Andy Rose and Marsha.

_____

_____

3. We saw squirrels rabbits and chipmunks in the park.

_____

_____

4. Bring the following a hat sunscreen and a jacket.

_____

_____

5. Snow ice and slush covered the road.

_____

_____

The Langston Times (continued)

Analyzing the Selection

Read the question below. Write complete sentences for your answer. Support your answer with evidence from the selection.

Compare what the children and adults thought of the new school.

_____

_____

_____

_____

_____

_____

_____

_____

_____

_____

_____

_____

_____

_____

_____

_____

_____

_____

Analyzing the Selection • *Assessment 1*

Name _____ Date _____

Eve did not play sports with the other girls in her school. She was smaller and thinner than they were. Eve liked to run and jump. She did not like sports like soccer or basketball. | 1-11 12-19 20-30 31-35

The town where Eve lived built a new school. There was a new gym and new activities. One day in gym class the teacher showed the girls how to do flips. Eve tried it. She was surprised because she did them so well. She liked it very much. | 36-44 45-54 55-64 65-73 74-83

The teacher told Eve that she was very talented. Maybe she could be a gymnast. This is a person who does lots of different jumps and flips. | 84-92 93-102 103-110

Eve joined a team. She practiced with other girls. It was hard work. Even so, Eve loved it. | 111-119 120-128

The part that Eve liked best was something called a balance beam. This is a narrow piece of wood. Eve walked on the wood and did flips and jumps. When she was finished, she did a flip from the beam to the floor. It was an amazing feeling, and Eve was pretty sure she found her sport. | 129-136 137-146 147-156 157-166 167-176 177-185

Evaluating Codes for Oral Fluency

| sky | (/) words read incorrectly |
| blue ^ sky | (^) Inserted word ([]) after the last word |

Reading Rate and Accuracy

Total Words Read	
Number of Errors	
Number of Correct Words Read per Minute (WCPM)	
Accuracy Rate	
(Number of Correct Words Read per Minute ÷ Total Words Read)	

Reading Prosody

	LOW	AVG.	HIGH
Decoding Ability	○	○	○
Pace	○	○	○
Syntax	○	○	○
Self-correction	○	○	○
Intonation	○	○	○

Oral Fluency Passage Information

Lexile Measure	470L
Mean Sentence Length	8.41
Mean Log Word Frequency	3.73
Word Count	185

Phonics: /ī/ spelled _igh, _ie, _y

Choose the word that completes each sentence. Write the word on the line.

fly   lie   high   style   pie

1. The dog likes to _____ under the shady tree.

2. The kite flew _____ in the sky.

3. The airplane will _____ from Ohio to Oregon.

4. My favorite dessert is cherry _____.

5. That artist has a unique _____ of painting.

Phonics: /ī/ spelled i, i_e

Unscramble the following words. Write the /ī/ spelling pattern on the second line.

6. d k i n _____

7. e i l m _____

8. h i l c d _____

9. e i n n _____

10. d i f n _____

The Stranger and the Soup

Vocabulary

Read each item. Fill in the correct answer.

1. What does the word *gasp* mean in this sentence?
People *gasp* when they see that circus trick.
- (A) stand and clap
- (B) breathe in suddenly
- (C) laugh out loud
- (D) sing along with the performer

2. What is a synonym for *simmer* in this sentence?
The vegetables had to *simmer* for a little while.
- (A) cook
- (B) dry
- (C) rest
- (D) wait

3. What does the word *well* most likely mean in this sentence?
Water for the farm came from a *well*.
- (A) a shallow bay
- (B) a metal tank
- (C) a big river
- (D) a deep hole

4. What does the word *sighed* mean in this sentence?
Carson *sighed* and bent down to clean up the mess.
- (A) let out a deep breath
- (B) giggled
- (C) hiccuped
- (D) made a funny face

5. What is a synonym for *seasoning* in this sentence?
The food had different kinds of *seasoning*.
- (A) cooking
- (B) wrapping
- (C) spices
- (D) shapes

The Stranger and the Soup (continued)

Comprehension

**Read the following items carefully and fill in the correct answer.
You may look back at the selection to answer the questions.**

1. The following question has two parts. First, answer **Part A**.
   Then, answer **Part B**.

   Part A What kind of person do you think Isabel is?
   - (A) afraid of strangers
   - (B) angry with her mother
   - (C) kind and caring
   - (D) a very good cook

   Part B Which sentence from the story **best** supports your
   answer for **Part A**?
   - (A) Isabel's mother shook her head.
   - (B) "But, Mamá, shouldn't we always try to help someone in
     need?" said Isabel.
   - (C) As she watched the man ask at door after door, she saw
     that her mother was right.
   - (D) Isabel's mother frowned up at the man.

2. When did Isabel discover the truth about the stone?
   - (A) when she first saw the stranger
   - (B) when winter was over
   - (C) when she tasted the soup
   - (D) when the stranger pulled out the stone

3. How did the villagers feel about the stranger after they ate
   the feast?
   - (A) They still did not trust him.
   - (B) They were happy to see him go.
   - (C) They wanted to go with him.
   - (D) They wanted him to stay.

The Stranger and the Soup (continued)

Comprehension

4. Which of these is an example of sensory details?
   - (A) want to help the stranger
   - (C) the most wonderful smell
   - (B) in a few minutes
   - (D) meet in the plaza

5. Who is telling this story?
   - (A) someone who knows the stranger
   - (B) Senhora Silva
   - (C) Isabel's mother
   - (D) someone not in the story

Read the following items carefully. Answer the questions.

6. Read each sentence. Choose the word that best completes the sentence.

   The stranger cooked in the _____.
   - **a.** plaza
   - **b.** garden
   - **c.** kitchen

   The first thing in the pot was the _____.
   - **a.** onion
   - **b.** stone
   - **c.** carrot

   Senhor Silva wanted to add _____.
   - **a.** seasoning
   - **b.** cabbage
   - **c.** garlic

7. Why was it so unusual to see the visitor?

   _____

8. How did the villagers survive the hard winter?

   _____

9. At the end of the story, did Isabel think the stone was magical?

   _____

10. Why had the villagers stopped talking to one another?

    _____

The Stranger and the Soup (continued)

Grammar, Usage, and Mechanics

Read each item. Choose the verb that correctly completes the sentence.

1. The sun _____ on the high desert.
   - (A) shine
   - (B) shone
   - (C) shines
   - (D) shining

2. Clouds _____ by on soft breezes.
   - (A) floats
   - (B) float
   - (C) floating
   - (D) floater

3. Just one bird _____ singing.
   - (A) are
   - (B) can
   - (C) am
   - (D) is

4. I _____ my bike everyday after school.
   - (A) ride
   - (B) rides
   - (C) ridden
   - (D) riding

5. The songs of spring _____ come at last.
   - (A) are
   - (B) has
   - (C) have
   - (D) is

The Stranger and the Soup (continued)
Analyzing the Selection

Read the question below. Write complete sentences for your answer. Support your answer with evidence from the selection.

How did the stranger change the village?

_____

_____

_____

_____

_____

_____

_____

_____

_____

_____

_____

_____

_____

_____

_____

_____

_____

Teacher Directions: Duplicate this page for each student you choose to assess. Make one copy of the Unit 3 Lesson 5 Oral Fluency Assessment found on page 235 for students to read from.

The oak tree was taller than any other tree in the forest. It had large green leaves. Many birds built nests in its branches. A fir tree stood beside the oak tree. One day, the oak tree spoke to the fir tree. "I am the biggest tree, so I am the most important." The green fir tree did not answer. It just sighed as a little breeze blew by.

> 1-10
> 11-19
> 20-29
> 30-40
> 41-52
> 53-61
> 62-69

Then fall came. The oak tree's leaves turned red and gold. "I am the most beautiful tree in the forest," it said. The fir tree still said nothing.

> 70-77
> 78-88
> 89-97

Then the cold winds blew. The oak tree's beautiful leaves turned brown and fell off. They blew away leaving no trace behind. Its branches were bare. "Oh, my goodness," said the oak tree. "I'm not as pretty as you anymore. You are still green, and I am bare."

> 98-106
> 107-115
> 116-123
> 124-134
> 135-144
> 145-146

The green fir tree smiled as the little forest animals hid under its full branches to get out of the cold. The fir tree finally answered the oak. "Each of us has a job to do. Each of us is beautiful in our own way."

> 147-156
> 157-168
> 169-179
> 180-191

Evaluating Codes for Oral Fluency

sky	(/) words read incorrectly
blue ^ sky	(^) Inserted word ([ ]) after the last word

Reading Rate and Accuracy

Total Words Read	
Number of Errors	
Number of Correct Words Read per Minute (WCPM)	
Accuracy Rate	
(Number of Correct Words Read per Minute ÷ Total Words Read)	

Reading Prosody

	LOW	AVG.	HIGH
Decoding Ability	○	○	○
Pace	○	○	○
Syntax	○	○	○
Self-correction	○	○	○
Intonation	○	○	○

Oral Fluency Passage Information

Lexile Measure	480L
Mean Sentence Length	8.30
Mean Log Word Frequency	3.68
Word Count	191

Night Shift
Vocabulary

Read each item. Fill in the correct answer.

1. What does the word *assemble* mean in this sentence?
Aunt Ellie will help me *assemble* this model airplane.
(A) take apart
(B) put together
(C) break open
(D) draw

2. What is a synonym for *change* in this sentence?
The worker will *change* the speed of the motor.
(A) avoid
(B) collect
(C) bruise
(D) adjust

3. What does the word *port* mean in this sentence?
The *port* is busy when ocean liners dock.
(A) an opening in a fence
(B) a canal beside a river
(C) a place for ships
(D) an old building

4. What does the word *maneuverable* mean in this sentence?
The fridge isn't *maneuverable* in this tiny kitchen.
(A) easily moved
(B) very shiny
(C) hard to use
(D) new

5. What does the word *perishable* mean in this sentence?
Put the *perishable* things in the refrigerator.
(A) already cooked
(B) ready to be eaten
(C) easily spoiled
(D) just bought

Night Shift (continued)
Comprehension

Read the following items carefully and fill in the correct answer. You may look back at the selection to answer the questions.

1. The following question has two parts. First, answer **Part A**. Then, answer **Part B**.

   Part A Which of these tells how the author feels about people who work the night shift?
   - Ⓐ They sometimes make a mess.
   - Ⓑ They write about their work all day.
   - Ⓒ They do interesting work.
   - Ⓓ They wish they were in bed.

   Part B Which sentence from the selection **best** supports your answer for **Part A**?
   - Ⓐ What a mess!
   - Ⓑ ... wishing you didn't have to go to bed ...
   - Ⓒ ... write about the news all day ...
   - Ⓓ ... doing all sorts of interesting things ...

2. Which phrase describes how the tugboat captain moves the trawler?
   - Ⓐ gently nudges
   - Ⓑ sturdy tugboat
   - Ⓒ unwieldy trawler
   - Ⓓ run aground

3. What is the result of mending the broken highway?
   - Ⓐ rush hour
   - Ⓒ delicious bagels
   - Ⓑ a traffic bottleneck
   - Ⓓ roads are empty

Night Shift (continued)

Comprehension

4. What is the jam in the printing plant?
- Ⓐ Reporters didn't finish their stories.
- Ⓑ The paper has to be folded and bundled
- Ⓒ It is too dark to see in the building.
- Ⓓ Paper is stuck in the press.

5. Which of these is an example of alliteration?
- Ⓐ street sweeper swishes
- Ⓒ revamp the windows
- Ⓑ store is closed
- Ⓓ sculptures are wobbling

Read the following items carefully. Answer the questions.

6. Match a key phrase with the worker to which it refers.

Street Sweeper	they choose the songs
Window Dresser	this job is about protecting
Late-Night Radio DJ	swishes along
Security guard	a mannequin dressed

7. Why is the light on for the nocturnal animals?

_____

_____

8. What happens at the end of the night shift?

_____

_____

9. How does the night shift worker make it hard for another worker?

_____

_____

10. Where is a hawk's nest mentioned in the selection, and why?

_____

_____

Comprehension • *Assessment 1*

Night Shift (continued)

Analyzing the Selection

Read the question below. Write complete sentences for your answer. Support your answer with evidence from the selection.

How do night shift workers affect what goes on during the day?

_____

_____

_____

_____

_____

_____

_____

_____

_____

_____

_____

_____

_____

_____

_____

_____

_____

_____

Name _____ **Date** _____

It was early in the day. The sun was not up yet,	1-12
so it was still dark. Pat and Lou huddled close	13-22
together. They were trying to keep warm, but they	23-31
didn't mind the cold.	32-35
They watched the people fill the huge balloon	36-43
with hot air. Then they saw the balloon rise	44-52
above the basket. It looked like a large red light	53-62
bulb. They thought that this must be the most	63-71
interesting job in the world.	72-76
Then the big moment came. The pilot waved to	77-85
them, and Pat and Lou walked toward him. This	86-94
would be their first ride in a hot air balloon. They	95-105
felt both nervous and excited.	106-110
Pat helped Lou into the basket, and then she	111-119
climbed in herself. She and Lou smiled at their	120-128
parents who stood nearby. They were all a bit	129-137
scared. The pilot said not to worry because	138-145
everything would be just fine.	146-150
The pilot turned on a burner. More air went into	151-160
the balloon. The basket they were in started going	161-169
up into the sky. The people holding the rope let go,	170-180
and the three of them looked down as the ground	181-190
seemed to move away. They were flying!	191-197

Evaluating Codes for Oral Fluency

sky	(/) words read incorrectly
blue ^ sky	(^) Inserted word () after the last word

Reading Rate and Accuracy

Total Words Read	
Number of Errors	
Number of Correct Words Read per Minute (WCPM)	
Accuracy Rate	
(Number of Correct Words Read per Minute ÷ Total Words Read)	

Reading Prosody

	LOW	AVG.	HIGH
Decoding Ability	○	○	○
Pace	○	○	○
Syntax	○	○	○
Self-correction	○	○	○
Intonation	○	○	○

Oral Fluency Passage Information

Lexile Measure	490L
Mean Sentence Length	9.38
Mean Log Word Frequency	3.88
Word Count	197

Phonics: /ā/ spelled *ai_, _ay, a, a_e*

Read each sentence. Choose the word that best completes the sentence.

1. Will you _____ until I am ready?

   a. wait **b.** wat **c.** wayt

2. The wind made the tree _____ back and forth.

   a. swaye **b.** sway **c.** swai

3. I live in the _____ of California.

   a. stat **b.** stait **c.** state

4. Dad likes to wear an _____ when he cooks.

   a. apron **b.** aperon **c.** aipron

5. The picture _____ is made of wood.

   a. frayme **b.** fraim **c.** frame

Phonics: /ē/ spelled _ie_, _y, _ey, ea

Read each sentence. Choose the word that best completes the sentence.

6. Ben took a _____ of the votes.

   a. tally   **b.** talle   **c.** tallea

7. How much _____ will the ticket cost?

   a. mone   **b.** money   **c.** monie

8. The _____ of light was bright.

   a. beme   **b.** beem   **c.** beam

9. The _____ robbed the bank.

   a. theaf   **b.** theef   **c.** thief

10. The _____ scratched its head.

    a. monkea   **b.** monkey   **c.** monkee

Phonics: /f/ spelled *ph*, /m/ spelled *_mb* and Silent Letters

Read each sentence. Fill in the bubble under the word that best completes the sentence and is spelled correctly.

11. Sam used a _____ to untangle his hair.

cam   com   comb

○   ○   ○

12. Kurt will take a _____ of the statue.

foto   photo   futo

○   ○   ○

13. A baby cow is called a _____.

calf   caff   caf

○   ○   ○

14. Mina hurt her _____.

rhist   rist   wrist

○   ○   ○

15. The _____ fixed the leaky pipe.

plubber   plumber   plumr

○   ○   ○

Phonics: /s/ spelled ce, ci_, cy and /j/ spelled gi_

Read each sentence. Choose the word that best completes the sentence.

16. The sprinter ran at a fast _____.

   a. pacie   **b.** pace   **c.** pase

17. I bought a box of _____ at a supply store.

   a. pencils   **b.** pencels   **c.** pencyls

18. The _____ was loud and busy.

   a. city   **b.** citee   **c.** cyte

19. I saw a _____ yacht in the harbor.

   a. fance   **b.** fanci   **c.** fancy

20. Alaska often has _____ weather.

   a. frigid   **b.** friged   **c.** frigd

Phonics: /ī/ spelled *i*, *_igh*, *_ie*, *_y*

Read each sentence. Choose the word that best completes the sentence.

21. My _____ socks squeezed my ankles.

  a. tite   **b.** tight   **c.** tighte

22. My favorite animal is a _____.

  a. tieger   **b.** tigher   **c.** tiger

23. My dad likes to eat _____ green tomatoes.

  a. friyed   **b.** fryed   **c.** fried

24. The baby will _____ when he is hungry.

  a. cry   **b.** cri   **c.** criie

25. The _____ light hurt my eyes.

  a. breight   **b.** bright   **c.** briht

Vocabulary

Name _____ **Date** _____ **Score** _____

Vocabulary

Read each item. Fill in the correct answer.

1. What is a synonym for *plant* in this sentence?
The workers walked toward the *plant* early in the morning.
(A) train
(B) factory
(C) meeting
(D) cabin

2. What does the word *nocturnal* mean in this sentence?
Our hamster is *nocturnal*, so he sleeps all day.
(A) thrashing
(B) falls asleep easily
(C) active at night
(D) splendid

3. What does the word *expired* mean in this sentence?
The milk is *expired*, so Dad went to the store.
(A) no longer usable
(B) crooked
(C) at the back
(D) studied closely

4. What does the word *fascination* most likely mean in this sentence?
Cora had a *fascination* with cats from an early age.
(A) little knowledge
(B) great fear
(C) special ability
(D) strong interest

5. What does the word *while* mean in this sentence?
Dad cooked *while* the family played outside.
(A) a great meal
(B) feeling lonely
(C) at the same time
(D) until it was finished

Vocabulary

6. What does the word *officials* mean in this sentence?

The *officials* ruled that the ball was out of bounds.

Ⓐ players
Ⓑ people in certain positions
Ⓒ journeys
Ⓓ areas beside water

7. What is a synonym for *revealing* in this sentence?

The scientists are *revealing* the new instrument.

Ⓐ repairing
Ⓑ constructing
Ⓒ displaying
Ⓓ enjoying

8. What does the word *seams* most likely mean in this sentence?

The *seams* in this metal tank are welded.

Ⓐ edges that people can see
Ⓑ parts that are on the outside
Ⓒ entrances into an area
Ⓓ places where things are joined

9. What does the word *shift* mean in this sentence?

The night *shift* starts around nine o'clock.

Ⓐ work time
Ⓑ singing group
Ⓒ wild animal
Ⓓ warm clothing

10. What is a synonym for *wilted* in this sentence?

The flowers *wilted* in the heat.

Ⓐ grew
Ⓑ climbed
Ⓒ drooped
Ⓓ released

Comprehension: Cold Read
Read the selection. Then answer the questions.

"Here's a question for you," said Mr. Dunn. "It's about your families and what they did long ago. What kinds of jobs did your family do long ago?"

None of the students knew how to answer the question. They were quiet for a minute. Some of them squirmed in their seats. The only who knew something about his family was Ted. He said that his family came from Maine, and that his grandfather worked on a fishing boat. His grandmother made clothes to keep people warm during cold weather.

"Let's do this," Mr. Dunn said. "Talk to your parents this week. Ask them about the jobs your families had long ago. Next week, we'll talk about what you find out."

"But for now," he added, "I'll tell you what I found out about my family. Maybe this will give you ideas about some questions you can ask."

"My parents were both teachers, so you can blame them if I don't do a good job," he said as a joke.

All the students laughed, especially Marsha. She lived next door to Mr. Dunn's parents. They said the same thing.

"There's one more thing," Mr. Dunn said. "I learned that more than a hundred years ago, my family members were slaves. After the Civil War, they became free, and they moved up north. They found jobs in Ohio, and they were able to save enough money to buy a farm. My uncle and his family still work the farm today."

GO ON

That week, the students did what Mr. Dunn asked. Some of them took notes, and some even recorded the stories that their parents told them. The next week they talked about what they had learned. They took turns telling about their families.

"My family comes from Italy," said Frank. "They had a little boat. They bought fruit in Sicily. Then they sailed to other parts of Italy. They sold the fruit there."

Rosa was next. "My family comes from Mexico. They lived in a tiny town. My grandmother made special pots from black clay. She was famous all over Mexico for the pots she made. We have one of the pots in our house. I liked the pot very much before, but now I like it even more because I know who made it."

"My family comes from China," Kim said. "Some of the men worked on the railroad when they came to the United States. This picture shows what they did. I would like to visit the place in this picture because there is a special railroad museum there."

All the students in the class took turns. They told their family stories, and some brought pictures or other things that showed what their families had done. When they finished, Mr. Dunn asked them how they felt. They all said they were proud of the jobs their families had done.

Comprehension

Read the following items carefully and answer the questions.

1. **Part A** How did the students change in the story?
   - Ⓐ They wanted to do the jobs their families did.
   - Ⓑ They didn't learn very much new.
   - Ⓒ They felt good about their families.
   - Ⓓ They decided to start a family history club.

   Part B Which sentence **best** supports your answer for **Part A**?
   - Ⓐ None of the students knew how to answer the question.
   - Ⓑ They were proud of the jobs their families had done.
   - Ⓒ Ask them about the jobs your families had long ago.
   - Ⓓ My uncle and his family still work the farm today.

2. What caused Rosa to like the pots in her house even more?
   - Ⓐ Because her grandmother was famous in Mexico.
   - Ⓑ She found out that the pots had been made with black clay.
   - Ⓒ She now is able to find the family's town in Mexico.
   - Ⓓ She learned that her grandmother had made them.

3. Which two students had families with similar jobs?
   - Ⓐ Frank and Ted
   - Ⓒ Kim and Frank
   - Ⓑ Rosa and Kim
   - Ⓓ Ted and Rosa

4. What was Ted's grandmother's job?
   - Ⓐ She was a teacher.
   - Ⓑ She worked on a fishing boat.
   - Ⓒ She made clothes to keep people warm.

5. Why did some of the students squirm?
   - Ⓐ They were impatient and wanted to answer right away.
   - Ⓑ They were embarrassed that they didn't know the answer.
   - Ⓒ They had things to share with the rest of the class.

Grammar, Usage, and Mechanics
Read each item. Fill in the correct answer.

1. Which of these sentences has correct punctuation?
   - Ⓐ Martha said Let's make a salad tonight.
   - Ⓑ Martha said "Let's make a salad tonight."
   - Ⓒ Martha said, "Let's make a salad tonight."
   - Ⓓ "Martha said let's make a salad tonight."

2. Which of these sentences has correct capitalization?
   - Ⓐ The Baseball game is on Saturday afternoon in Fairfax.
   - Ⓑ The baseball game is on Saturday afternoon in Fairfax.
   - Ⓒ The baseball game is on saturday afternoon in Fairfax.
   - Ⓓ The baseball Game is on Saturday afternoon in Fairfax.

3. Which of these sentences has correct capitalization?
   - Ⓐ We took a road trip to Oregon last july.
   - Ⓑ We took a road trip to oregon last July.
   - Ⓒ We took a road trip to oregon last july.
   - Ⓓ We took a road trip to Oregon last July.

4. Rewrite the sentence and put commas where they are needed.
   Stores hotels and restaurants lined the streets.

   _____

   _____

5. Rewrite the sentence and put a colon and commas where they are needed.
   The events are as follows softball awards and picnic.

   _____

   _____

Grammar, Usage, and Mechanics

6. In which sentence is the underlined word correct?
- Ⓐ The road gets a lot <u>wide</u> pretty soon.
- Ⓑ The road gets a lot <u>wider</u> pretty soon.
- Ⓒ The road gets a lot <u>widest</u> pretty soon.
- Ⓓ The road gets a lot <u>widely</u> pretty soon.

7. Choose the article that completes the sentence.
I have _____ blue backpack.
- Ⓐ a
- Ⓑ an
- Ⓒ the
- Ⓓ is

8. Choose the article that completes the sentence.
We climbed up _____ steps to the second floor.
- Ⓐ a
- Ⓑ an
- Ⓒ is
- Ⓓ the

9. Choose the verb that correctly completes the sentence.
A willow tree _____ by the pond.
- Ⓐ grow
- Ⓑ growing
- Ⓒ grows
- Ⓓ grown

10. Choose the verb that correctly completes the sentence.
The bear cubs _____ to play together.
- Ⓐ likes
- Ⓑ liking
- Ⓒ like
- Ⓓ likely

Spelling

Choose the correct way to spell the underlined word. If the underlined word is correct, choose the last answer, *Leave as is.* **Fill in the correct answer.**

1. Is it supposed to <u>rane</u> today?
   - Ⓐ rain
   - Ⓑ ran
   - Ⓒ raen
   - Ⓓ Leave as is.

2. Let's go <u>play</u> soccer.
   - Ⓐ playe
   - Ⓑ plae
   - Ⓒ pla
   - Ⓓ Leave as is.

3. Some horses were in the <u>feeld</u>.
   - Ⓐ feld
   - Ⓑ felde
   - Ⓒ field
   - Ⓓ Leave as is.

4. How much <u>mony</u> does this cost?
   - Ⓐ money
   - Ⓑ monee
   - Ⓒ monie
   - Ⓓ Leave as is.

5. This <u>graph</u> shows wins and losses.
   - Ⓐ graff
   - Ⓑ grafe
   - Ⓒ graf
   - Ⓓ Leave as is.

Spelling

6. Hand me that <u>com</u>, please.
   - (A) comme
   - (B) comb
   - (C) comp
   - (D) Leave as is.

7. The point of the <u>pencl</u> broke.
   - (A) pencil
   - (B) pensil
   - (C) penscil
   - (D) Leave as is.

8. A <u>larje</u> cow stood by the fence.
   - (A) lardje
   - (B) lardge
   - (C) large
   - (D) Leave as is.

9. The moon was full last <u>night</u>.
   - (A) nihgt
   - (B) nipht
   - (C) nitte
   - (D) Leave as is.

10. Let's <u>trie</u> to win this game.
    - (A) try
    - (B) trai
    - (C) tri
    - (D) Leave as is.

Teacher Directions: Duplicate this page for each student you choose to assess. Make one copy of the Unit 3 Oral Fluency Assessment found on page 237 for students to read from.

The day started out nice with a beautiful sunrise. | 1-9
It was a perfect day for taking a walk. There was a | 10-21
little breeze, and some clouds floated in the sky. | 22-30

Around noon, the sky got cloudier and the wind | 31-39
got stronger. The weather reporter said that a | 40-47
storm was coming in. Before long, it started to | 48-56
rain. There were booms of thunder and flashes of | 57-65
lightning. | 66

People went inside if they could find someplace | 67-74
nearby. Some people walking outside put up | 75-81
their umbrellas. The wind made it hard to hold an | 82-91
umbrella. Other people ran quickly to their cars to | 92-100
get out of the rain. | 101-105

Drivers on the highway had to slow down in their | 106-115
cars. The falling rain made it hard to see, and there | 116-126
were big puddles in the streets. When cars went | 127-135
by, people got splashed. Traffic was backed up | 136-143
for blocks. | 144-145

The river that flowed through town started to rise. | 146-154
Some people got dressed up in raincoats and hats. | 155-163
They walked over to the bridge so they could see | 164-173
the river. It was not dangerous, because the bridge | 174-182
was high and had been built well. | 183-189

After a while, the rain stopped, and the sun | 190-198
peeked through the clouds. The air smelled fresh | 199-206
and clean. Some people came outside and got a | 207-215
special treat. A beautiful rainbow spread across | 216-222
the sky. | 223-224

Evaluating Codes for Oral Fluency

sky	(/) words read incorrectly
blue ^ sky	(^) Inserted word (]) after the last word

Reading Rate and Accuracy

Total Words Read	
Number of Errors	
Number of Correct Words Read per Minute (WCPM)	
Accuracy Rate	
(Number of Correct Words Read per Minute ÷ Total Words Read)	

Reading Prosody

	LOW	AVG.	HIGH
Decoding Ability	○	○	○
Pace	○	○	○
Syntax	○	○	○
Self-correction	○	○	○
Intonation	○	○	○

Oral Fluency Passage Information

Lexile Measure	560L
Mean Sentence Length	9.74
Mean Log Word Frequency	3.77
Word Count	224

Name _____ **Date** _____ **Score** _____

Narrative Writing Task

Write a made-up story about life in the future. Include details and descriptive language so the reader will get a good picture of the future world. Be sure to use your imagination. When you write, remember to

- express your ideas clearly.
- include a beginning, middle, and ending.
- use correct grammar, spelling, punctuation, and capitalization.

_____

_____

_____

_____

_____

_____

_____

_____

_____

_____

_____

_____

_____

_____

_____

_____

_____

_____

Four Point Rubrics for Narrative Writing

Genre	1 Point	2 Points	3 Points	4 Points
Narrative Writing	Narrative has missing details or elements. Order and narrative structure are lacking. Plot is unclear. Character development is not apparent. Setting does not include descriptions of where and when the narrative is set. No real ending is evident.	Narrative includes plot outline and some descriptive details, but narrative structure is not entirely clear. Character development is minimal. Setting includes minimal descriptions of where and when the narrative is set. The narrative does not include an ending.	Narrative includes fairly well developed plot with descriptive details and other elements such as subplots that are integrated into the resolution. Narrative structure is clear. Characters are developed, though some characters may seem superficial. Setting includes descriptions of where and when the narrative is set. The narrative has an ending.	Narrative includes more complicated plot lines with varied timelines, flashbacks, or dual story lines. Narrative structure is well defined. Characters well defined throughout with unique qualities integral to the plot. Setting includes detailed descriptions of where and when the narrative is set. The narrative has a strong ending.
Narrative: Theme	No theme is apparent.	Superficial theme is included but not integrated.	A theme is expressed but not well developed.	The narrative fully develops a theme that expresses an underlying message beyond the narrative plot.
Writing Traits				
Audience	Displays little or no sense of audience.	Displays some sense of audience.	Writes with audience in mind throughout.	Displays a strong sense of audience. Engages audience.
Voice	The writing provides little sense of involvement or commitment. There is no evidence that the writer has chosen a suitable voice.	The writer's commitment to the topic seems inconsistent. A sense of the writer may emerge at times; however, the voice is either inappropriately personal or inappropriately impersonal.	A voice is present. The writer demonstrates commitment to the topic. In places, the writing is expressive, engaging, or sincere. Words and expressions are clear and precise.	The writer has chosen a voice appropriate for the topic, purpose, and audience. Unique style comes through. The writing is expressive, engaging, or sincere. Strong commitment to the topic.
Writing Conventions				
Conventions Overall	Numerous errors in usage, grammar, spelling, capitalization, and punctuation repeatedly distract the reader and make the text difficult to read. The reader finds it difficult to focus on the message.	The writing demonstrates limited control of standard writing conventions (punctuation, spelling, grammar, and usage). Errors sometimes impede readability.	The writing demonstrates control of standard writing conventions (punctuation, spelling, grammar, and usage). Minor errors, while perhaps noticeable, do not impede readability.	The writing demonstrates exceptionally strong control of standard writing conventions (punctuation, spelling, grammar, and usage) and uses them effectively to enhance communication. Errors are so few and so minor that the reader can easily skim over them.

Six Point Writing Rubrics

Use the following rubrics to assess student writing.

6 Points

The writing is focused, purposeful, and reflects insight into the writing situation. The paper conveys a sense of completeness and wholeness with adherence to the main idea, and its organizational pattern provides for a logical progression of ideas. The support is substantial, specific, relevant, concrete, and/or illustrative. The paper demonstrates a commitment to and an involvement with the subject, clarity in presentation of ideas, and may use creative writing strategies appropriate to the purpose of the paper. The writing demonstrates a mature command of language (word choice) with freshness of expression. Sentence structure is varied, and sentences are complete except when fragments are used purposefully. Few, if any, convention errors occur in mechanics, usage, and punctuation.

5 Points

The writing focuses on the topic, and its organizational pattern provides for a progression of ideas, although some lapses may occur. The paper conveys a sense of completeness or wholeness. The support is ample. The writing demonstrates a mature command of language, including precise word choice. There is variation in sentence structure, and, with rare exceptions, sentences are complete except when fragments are used purposefully. The paper generally follows the conventions of mechanics, usage, and spelling.

4 Points

The writing is generally focused on the topic but may include extraneous or loosely related material. An organizational pattern is apparent, although some lapses may occur. The paper exhibits some sense of completeness or wholeness. The support, including word choice, is adequate, although development may be uneven. There is little variation in sentence structure, and most sentences are complete. The paper generally follows the conventions of mechanics, usage, and spelling.

3 Points

The writing is generally focused on the topic but may include extraneous or loosely related material. An organizational pattern has been attempted, but the paper may lack a sense of completeness or wholeness. Some support is included, but development is erratic. Word choice is adequate but may be limited, predictable, or occasionally vague. There is little, if any, variation in sentence structure. Knowledge of the conventions of mechanics and usage is usually demonstrated, and commonly used words are usually spelled correctly.

2 Points

The writing is related to the topic but includes extraneous or loosely related material. Little evidence of an organizational pattern may be demonstrated, and the paper may lack a sense of completeness of wholeness. Development of support is inadequate or illogical. Word choice is limited, inappropriate, or vague. There is little, if any, variation in sentence structure, and gross errors in sentence structure may occur. Errors in basic conventions of mechanics and usage may occur, and commonly used words may be misspelled.

1 Point

The writing may only minimally address the topic. The paper is fragmentary or an incoherent listing of related ideas or sentences or both. Little, if any, development of support or an organizational pattern or both is apparent. Limited or inappropriate word choice may obscure meaning. Gross errors in sentence structure and usage may impede communication. Frequent and blatant errors may occur in the basic conventions of mechanics and usage, and commonly used words may be misspelled.

Unscorable

The paper is unscorable because

- the response is not related to what the prompt requested the student to do.
- the response is simply a rewording of the prompt.
- the response is a copy of a published work.
- the student refused to write.
- the response is illegible.

- the response is incomprehensible (words are arranged in such a way that no meaning is conveyed).
- the response contains an insufficient amount of writing to determine if the student was attempting to address the prompt.

Lesson and Unit Assessment

Unit 1 Class Assessment Record

Student Name	Lesson 1 pp. 23–29	Lesson 2 pp. 30–37	Lesson 3 pp. 38–46	Lesson 4 pp. 47–54	Lesson 5 pp. 55–62	Lesson 6 pp. 63–67	Unit 1 Assessment pp. 68–83

Lesson and Unit Assessment

Unit 2 Class Assessment Record

Student Name	Lesson 1 pp. 85–92	Lesson 2 pp. 93–100	Lesson 3 pp. 101–109	Lesson 4 pp. 110–117	Lesson 5 pp. 118–125	Lesson 6 pp. 126–130	Unit 2 Assessment pp. 131–145

Lesson and Unit Assessment

Unit 3 Class Assessment Record

Student Name	Lesson 1 pp. 147–154	Lesson 2 pp. 155–162	Lesson 3 pp. 163–171	Lesson 4 pp. 172–179	Lesson 5 pp. 180–187	Lesson 6 pp. 188–192	Unit 3 Assessment pp. 193–208

Assessment 1

Student Assessment Record

Name_____

Teacher _____ **Grade** _____

Unit/ Lesson	Assessment Name	Date	Number Possible	Number Right	%	Score

Lesson and Unit Assessment

Oral Fluency Assessment Record

Student Name	Date								

Comprehension Observation Log

Student _____ Date _____

Unit _____ Lesson _____ Selection Title _____

For each area of comprehension, note specific behaviors or indicators of student performance.

Interacts during reading by:

Asking questions _____

_____

Making predictions _____

_____

Retelling story parts (summarizes) _____

_____

Making connections _____

_____

Visualizing _____

Contributes to class discussion by:

Making comments about the selection _____

Listening to other stories and unit theme _____

_____

Changes Since Last Observation
_____
_____
_____
_____
_____

Assessment 1

Mice like to live near people. There is a reason for this. People live in houses, and they cook and eat in their houses. This is perfect for mice because it means they have places to live. They also have food to eat.

There are many different kinds of mice. Some live near people, but others live in the wild. They don't like living near people. They know how to find food and make a home without people.

In the wild, mice eat different kinds of food. They like seeds and nuts. They are very smart, and they are also very careful. That is because other animals like to eat mice.

Many animals live in colonies. These are groups of animals. Ants live in colonies. They dig tunnels under the ground. The tunnels go far into the ground. They have spaces for ants to sleep. There are spaces for food. There are even spaces for ant eggs and babies.

Prairie dogs also live in colonies. These are animals that live on the western plains. They dig holes in the ground. A prairie dog colony can have ten or more families.

The holes that prairie dogs make are very important. They help the animals stay warm in winter and cool in summer. They also keep rain from flooding the colony. Prairie dogs are smart, but they are also cute. People love to watch them poke their heads out of their holes.

Many animals work together. A good example is bees. When a bee finds a good flower, it goes back to the hive. The bee does a special dance. The way it dances tells the other bees where the flowers are.

The name of the place where a bee lives is a hive. A bee hive shows how good bees are at working together. They all help to build the hive. It would be impossible for one bee to make a hive.

Bees make their hives in holes in the ground or in trees. Sometimes people help them. They make special boxes. The bees make a hive in the box.

The inside of a bee hive is amazing. It is made up of little wax boxes with six sides called cells. The cells form a honey comb. The bees make the cells of wax. The inside of each cell is filled with honey.

A bat is a very unusual animal. It looks like a mouse, but it flies like a bird. It has fur like an animal but wings like a bird. Isn't that amazing?

Bats don't build nests like birds. They live in caves, under bridges, and in other dark places. They do this for protection. In a cave, bats are safe from bad weather or animals that might eat them. Best of all, the bats did not have to build their home. They just moved right in.

Most bats eat flying insects. The bats come out at night and fly around. When they find a tasty flying bug, they gobble it up.

How do bats travel around at night, and how do they find bugs? Bats make a squeaky noise. This special noise bounces off a tree or bug. Bats hear the echo of the sound. That way they can avoid flying into trees and can also find food.

Ice hockey is a popular sport in many places. Most of these places are cold, but some are warm. You might be surprised to learn how many warm places have hockey teams.

In places like Canada or the northern United States, people like to play hockey outside. A frozen pond or lake is perfect. A few friends show up with skates, sticks, and a puck. The game is on.

Players in Canada may have invented ice hockey. It is the country's national winter sport. Boys and girls grow up playing hockey. Many of them dream of becoming professional players. Even if they don't become professionals, they will continue to play as grown-ups.

Hockey has spread all over the world. Some of the best players come from countries like Norway, Sweden, and Finland. These are countries with cold weather and lots of frozen ponds or lakes to play on.

But what about the rest of the world? How do they play? The answer is easy. They play inside. Ice arenas can be found all over the world.

Hiking is a wonderful activity. It is good exercise and lets you enjoy nature in a very special way. Best of all, you can hike almost anywhere, including big cities.

When people think of hiking, they usually think of forests and mountains. These are both good places to hike. But there are lots of other options. You can hike along beaches, beside rivers, and on the shores of lakes. Some trails go through swamps. Others take you through the desert. In Hawaii, you can even hike near volcanoes.

When you hike, it is good to know where you are. People often use their smart phones or other electronic devices to follow a trail. Other people like to do it the old-fashioned way. They use a map made of paper. They think there is something special about holding a map in their hand. The people love figuring out where they are.

One of the most important parts of a hike is looking up, down, and all around. There is always something interesting to see. There are rocks on the ground and birds in the sky. In between there are trees, hills, and other wonderful sights.

Long ago, people ate only raw food. Cooking had to wait until people learned to use fire. But it was a great idea. It makes many kinds of food safer by killing germs. Cooking also makes food easier for your body to use.

When you digest food, you turn it into something that your body can use. After you eat food, it goes to your stomach. Here and in other parts of your body it is turned into energy. The food is used by your body to make you strong and smart.

Cooking allowed people to eat more and different things. People did not starve because they had many things to eat.

Here's a surprising thing about cooking. It helped to make people smarter. People sat around the cooking fire. They talked to each other. They learned from one another. They became friends. They learned to share food. All of this helped to make people into a strong tribe.

Probably the best thing about cooking is that it made food taste better. At first, people just put meat in a fire and let it burn. After a while, people learned how to make pots. They could mix different foods together and cook them. The food tasted wonderful, and the world was changed forever.

A group of people stood around a puddle on the ground. From the puddle spilled a small stream of water. The puddle and stream had come from nowhere. During the night, a spring had appeared in the park, and no one knew what had caused it.

The stream flowed through the park. It ran down the slope and between trees, soon joining up with another stream.

The park ranger walked up to the group. She looked at the spring and said, "Welcome back." The people were curious. They asked her what she was talking about.

"A long time ago, there was a spring here," she said. "Then we had many dry years. This year we have had a lot of rain and snow. Some people thought the spring had dried up, but others thought it was sleeping. I guess they were right. The spring was taking a nap. It was waiting for the rain."

The lake was long and deep. It looked like it could have been made by humans. But that is not how it was made. A glacier did it.

Thousands of years ago, the area was covered by ice. It was hundreds of feet thick in spots. The weight of the ice was great. It pressed down on the ground so hard that it cut a big hole.

The ice grew thicker because Earth was colder than the ice. Earth started to warm up, and the giant ice sheet melted. Eventually, it disappeared. It left behind gashes in the ground. Sometimes they filled with water and became lakes.

Around the lake there were also big rocks called boulders. These rocks looked different from the other rocks in the area. That's because they were different. They were brought to the area by the glaciers from places far away. The rocks got stuck in the glacier. They moved when the glacier moved. When it melted, they stayed where they were dropped.

It was Claude's first visit to California. He was staying with his cousins who were about his age. He was having a great time visiting places he had never been.

One day they were in a forest near the Pacific Ocean. All of a sudden, the ground began to shake. It shook so hard that they all fell over.

"What was that?" asked Claude while he was still on the ground.

"That was a little earthquake called a tremor," answered Aunt Lillian. "Why don't we all stay on the ground for a few minutes to make sure it's over."

Claude had no problem with that. In fact, he was afraid to get up. He was also amazed that everyone else seemed so calm.

Uncle Phil noticed the look on Claude's face. He said, "We're used to it. Tremors happen here pretty often. They don't cause damage. We are in a safe place here. There are no buildings around. Your cousin Veronica will tell you all about the geology here."

People have learned how to live with earthquakes. We now make buildings that are safer than they were before. None of them are perfectly safe. But they are better than in the past.

Tall skyscrapers go hundreds of feet into the air. These buildings are made safe in an odd way. They are built on a special foundation. This is the part of the building that is way under the ground. When there is an earthquake, the building slides back and forth. It moves just a little bit. It doesn't fall over. The people inside are safe.

Many buildings are made of concrete. We can make the concrete stronger. There are steel rods in the concrete. This happens when the concrete is still soft. The rods keep the building from collapsing during an earthquake. If the concrete cracks, the rods will help to hold the building together.

In some parts of the world, people make their houses out of very light natural materials. When an earthquake hits, the houses shake. They usually don't fall. If they do, the houses are easy to fix.

Wayne and his friend, Jess, were playing in the park. Wayne saw a strange rock. He picked it up. It was black and shiny. He brought the rock home to show to his father.

"That's coal," Dad said. Then he asked, "Would you like to learn more about it? You might be surprised to learn how coal was mined and used here."

The next day, Dad took Wayne and Jess to a museum. It was filled with information about coal. One display case showed how coal was formed. It comes from swamps. Dead plants rotted in the swamps. Slowly, the rotting plants and other matter turned to coal.

People used to use coal to heat their homes. It is still used to make electricity and for other things. People are also trying to find ways to use coal that are safer for the environment.

As they left, Wayne's father said, "So how did you like our trip?"

"It was great," Wayne said. "I had no idea how important coal was and where it came from. It's hard to believe that where we live now was once a swamp surrounded by forests."

For most people, volcanoes are a little scary. They are exploding mountains from which lava flows. Everything near the volcano is destroyed. That is true for some volcanoes. But others are a little different and much less dangerous.

An active volcano is one that is still able to explode. These are dangerous. They don't explode very often. Even so, people are very careful.

Some volcanoes are dormant. That means they can still explode, but they probably won't. If they do, it will happen only rarely.

A third kind of volcano is an extinct volcano. This is one that has stopped exploding. It will probably never explode again. Most of the time, an extinct volcano looks just like other mountains.

In New Mexico, there is a mountain called Mt. Taylor. It is an extinct volcano. Most people don't know that. All they see is a beautiful mountain. It sits in the middle of the desert. It has snow on top in the winter, and people like to use snowshoes to get to the top. In the summer, hikers from all over come to enjoy the beautiful scenery. When they get to the top, they can see for hundreds of miles all around.

Earth changes in many ways. Some are small, and you don't see them. Others are large. Different things cause these changes.

One thing that causes changes is water. Think about a rain storm. Some of the water flows quickly down hills. It goes fast if the hills are steep, and the flowing water moves dirt and rocks. When this happens, deep cuts can be formed. One type of cut is called a valley. Another is a canyon. Moving water made one of our country's most famous sights. It's the Grand Canyon, and it is more than a mile deep.

Wind can also change things on Earth. Sand can be found on a beach or in the desert. When the wind blows, the sand moves around. It forms hills called dunes. Sometimes these hills can be hundreds of feet high.

There was a knock at the door.

"Can you get that?" Mom said. She was with the baby.

Brian opened the door, and saw that his neighbor, Mr. Green, was there.

"Hi, Mr. Green," Brian said.

"Brian, you're just the person I wanted to talk to," Mr. Green said. He explained that he had to go out of town and needed someone to feed his pets while he was gone. He asked Brian to do it.

"No problem," Brian said. "I like animals, and I would really enjoy it."

The next day Brian went to Mr. Green's house. First he fed the fish. Brian liked all their bright colors. He laughed when they raced to catch the fish food as it floated on the water.

Next Brian put food and water in the cat's dish. Daisy the cat was curled up on the sofa. Brian played with Daisy, who loved to chase a colorful ball. Then he petted her. Daisy purred loudly.

"This is a great job," Brian thought. "I hope I can do it every week."

When I got to school, I was in for a surprise. My teacher said the class was going on a field trip. She said we would visit a woodcarver's shop.

A special bus took the class to the shop. The shop was nice and cozy. It had a large wood stove. Shelves along the walls were filled with carvings. Even the tables and benches in the shop were carved.

We sat down and watched one woodcarver while he worked. He showed us how to slice, whittle, and drill. He showed us how to make notches as well.

A second one did something different. She was looking at pieces of wood. She showed us how she chose wood for her carvings.

I asked if there were any of their finished pieces we could see. The first woodcarver smiled proudly. Then he pointed at a large carving of a crane. He told us it was going to a gift shop a few blocks away. I decided to visit that shop soon. I really liked the crane. It would be a perfect gift for my parents.

It was a rainy day, and there wasn't anything interesting to do. Lena's uncle thought they should build a kite. Lena had no idea you could build a kite, but she thought it was a great idea.

Lena's uncle found some thin sticks to build the frame. Next, he put tissue paper over the frame. The paper had to be glued down. It would take time for the glue to dry. Lena's aunt made lunch. It was the perfect way to wait for the glue to dry.

Lena found some old pieces of cloth for the kite's tail. She helped her uncle rip the cloth into strips. Then she tied the shorter strips onto a string. This would be the tail for the kite.

They attached the tail to the kite. Then they got a ball of string. Lena's uncle tied the string to the kite, and he and Lena walked outside. They stopped and looked around. The air was still. The leaves on the tree were not moving.

"We're missing one thing," said Lena's uncle. "There is no wind. And we can't do anything about that!"

Eve did not play sports with the other girls in her school. She was smaller and thinner than they were. Eve liked to run and jump. She did not like sports like soccer or basketball.

The town where Eve lived built a new school. There was a new gym and new activities. One day in gym class the teacher showed the girls how to do flips. Eve tried it. She was surprised because she did them so well. She liked it very much.

The teacher told Eve that she was very talented. Maybe she could be a gymnast. This is a person who does lots of different jumps and flips.

Eve joined a team. She practiced with other girls. It was hard work. Even so, Eve loved it.

The part that Eve liked best was something called a balance beam. This is a narrow piece of wood. Eve walked on the wood and did flips and jumps. When she was finished, she did a flip from the beam to the floor. It was an amazing feeling, and Eve was pretty sure she found her sport.

The oak tree was taller than any other tree in the forest. It had large green leaves. Many birds built nests in its branches. A fir tree stood beside the oak tree. One day, the oak tree spoke to the fir tree. "I am the biggest tree, so I am the most important." The green fir tree did not answer. It just sighed as a little breeze blew by.

Then fall came. The oak tree's leaves turned red and gold. "I am the most beautiful tree in the forest," it said. The fir tree still said nothing.

Then the cold winds blew. The oak tree's beautiful leaves turned brown and fell off. They blew away leaving no trace behind. Its branches were bare. "Oh, my goodness," said the oak tree. "I'm not as pretty as you anymore. You are still green, and I am bare."

The green fir tree smiled as the little forest animals hid under its full branches to get out of the cold. The fir tree finally answered the oak. "Each of us has a job to do. Each of us is beautiful in our own way."

It was early in the day. The sun was not up yet, so it was still dark. Pat and Lou huddled close together. They were trying to keep warm, but they didn't mind the cold.

They watched the people fill the huge balloon with hot air. Then they saw the balloon rise above the basket. It looked like a large red light bulb. They thought that this must be the most interesting job in the world.

Then the big moment came. The pilot waved to them, and Pat and Lou walked toward him. This would be their first ride in a hot air balloon. They felt both nervous and excited.

Pat helped Lou into the basket, and then she climbed in herself. She and Lou smiled at their parents who stood nearby. They were all a bit scared. The pilot said not to worry because everything would be just fine.

The pilot turned on a burner. More air went into the balloon. The basket they were in started going up into the sky. The people holding the rope let go, and the three of them looked down as the ground seemed to move away. They were flying!

The day started out nice with a beautiful sunrise. It was a perfect day for taking a walk. There was a little breeze, and some clouds floated in the sky.

Around noon, the sky got cloudier and the wind got stronger. The weather reporter said that a storm was coming in. Before long, it started to rain. There were booms of thunder and flashes of lightning.

People went inside if they could find someplace nearby. Some people walking outside put up their umbrellas. The wind made it hard to hold an umbrella. Other people ran quickly to their cars to get out of the rain.

Drivers on the highway had to slow down in their cars. The falling rain made it hard to see, and there were big puddles in the streets. When cars went by, people got splashed. Traffic was backed up for blocks.

The river that flowed through town started to rise. Some people got dressed up in raincoats and hats. They walked over to the bridge so they could see the river. It was not dangerous, because the bridge was high and had been built well.

After a while, the rain stopped, and the sun peeked through the clouds. The air smelled fresh and clean. Some people came outside and got a special treat. A beautiful rainbow spread across the sky.

Ann was going to see her grandmother, and she was bringing her a surprise.

Mother said, "Do you think Grandmother will like her new friend?"

"I think so," said Ann. "She likes cats."

A little kitten was sitting in Ann's lap. The kitten was purring softly.

"Will you be sad when you give Fluffy to Grandmother?" asked Mother.

"No," said Ann. "We have our own cats, and I want Grandmother to have a friend."

Ann's mother stopped the car. She got out of the car and opened the door for Ann.

Ann got out of the car. She carried Fluffy in her arms. They walked to the porch, and Mother knocked on the door. Ann couldn't wait to see Grandmother's face.

Answer Key

Diagnostic Assessment
Phonemic Awareness ◆ pp. 1–4

1. A
2. C
3. B
4. C
5. C
6. A
7. C
8. D
9. C
10. B
11. B
12. C
13. A
14. A
15. B
16. C
17. C
18. C
19. B
20. C

Phonics and Decoding ◆ pp. 5–8

1. A
2. B
3. C
4. C
5. C
6. A
7. B
8. A
9. B
10. C
11. A
12. C
13. A
14. A
15. B
16. D
17. C
18. B
19. B
20. A

Spelling ◆ pp. 10–11

1. C
2. A
3. A
4. D
5. B
6. C
7. B
8. D
9. A
10. C
11. A
12. C
13. A
14. C
15. B

Vocabulary ◆ pp. 12–14

1. C
2. C
3. A
4. D
5. B
6. A
7. A
8. B
9. D
10. C
11. B
12. D
13. D
14. C
15. C

Comprehension ◆ pp. 15–22

1. A
2. B
3. A
4. C
5. A
6. B
7. C
8. C
9. A
10. C
11. B
12. A
13. C
14. A
15. C
16. B
17. A
18. C
19. A
20. C

Unit 1 • Lesson 1 Phonics ◆ p. 23

1. each
2. with
3. ship
4. what
5. farm

Vocabulary ◆ p. 24

1. B
2. C
3. D
4. A
5. B

Comprehension ◆ pp. 25–26

1. Part A: C   Part B: B
2. D
3. A
4. C
5. B
6. Possible answers: timber, cement, bricks
7. Possible answer: They brought some furniture.
8. Possible answer: They wanted to thank their friends and relatives.
9. Possible answers: Pa helped Ann to mix cement. Ma held the shoe string for Mick to cut. Mary fetched bricks for Grandpa. Mary and Tim made the windows and doors.

Answer Key

10. Possible answer: Pa is a problem-solver. Pa develops a plan to protect his family.

Grammar, Usage, and Mechanics ◆ *p. 27*
1. C
2. A
3. D
4. B
5. C

Unit 1 • Lesson 2
Phonics ◆ *pp. 30–31*
1. Closed
2. Not Closed
3. Closed
4. Closed
5. Not Closed
6. edge
7. back
8. catch
9. bridge
10. rock

Vocabulary ◆ *p. 32*
1. D
2. A
3. B
4. C
5. B

Comprehension ◆ *pp. 33–34*
1. Part A: D   Part B: C
2. D
3. B
4. B
5. C
6. Possible answer: The headings help inform the reader about the main ideas.
7. Possible answer: Ladybugs probably eat aphids, but ants protect aphids.

8. Possible answer: The aphids sucked so much juice out of the plant that it died. They need a new plant for food.
9. Possible answer: It is warmer under the ground in winter, so the eggs don't freeze. The ants can protect the eggs underground from predators.
10. drink

Grammar, Usage, and Mechanics ◆ *p. 35*
1. A
2. C
3. D
4. B
5. C

Unit 1 • Lesson 3
Phonics ◆ *pp. 38–40*
1. when
2. chair
3. hard
4. thank
5. wash
6. duck
7. judge
8. kick
9. watch
10. badge
11. jumped
12. bells
13. boxes
14. turkey
15. window

Vocabulary ◆ *p. 41*
1. C
2. A
3. B
4. D
5. D

Comprehension ◆ *pp. 42–43*
1. Part A: D   Part B: B
2. C
3. A
4. B
5. B
6. Possible answer: The Beasts were big, burly, and brawny while the Birds were quick and nimble.
7. Bat would be able to play more in the game.
8. Possible answer: The wings were folded so far back that you couldn't see them. He would look like a Beast.
9. Answers may vary.
10. Answers may vary.

Grammar, Usage, and Mechanics ◆ *p. 44*
1. C
2. A
3. B
4. D
5. B

Unit 1 • Lesson 4
Phonics ◆ *pp. 47–48*
1. rang
2. think
3. asking
4. bank
5. song
6. seven
7. hello
8. apple
9. alone
10. family

Answer Key

Vocabulary ◆ *p. 49*
1. B
2. C
3. A
4. B
5. D

Comprehension ◆ *pp. 50–51*
1. Part A: C   Part B: B
2. D
3. A
4. B
5. C
6. Possible answers for Big Bear: roared, bellowed Possible answers for Little Mouse: disappointed, slumped
7. Possible answer: He came up with a good idea.
8. Possible answer: Pretty Feathered Eagle made the wings from the leather cover of a drum.
9. Possible answer: The animals could not work together and fought among themselves.
10. Possible answer: He heard the drumbeats and followed them into the woods.

Grammar, Usage, and Mechanics ◆ *p. 52*
1. B
2. D
3. A
4. C
5. B

Unit 1 • Lesson 5
Phonics ◆ *pp. 55–56*
1. dirt
2. butter
3. hurry
4. first
5. turtle
6. fort
7. sore
8. born
9. store
10. north

Vocabulary ◆ *p. 57*
1. A
2. D
3. B
4. C
5. C

Comprehension ◆ *pp. 58–59*
1. Part A: C Part B: A
2. D
3. B
4. B
5. C
6. Answers may vary.
7. cross-checked
8. Possible answer: He knew that the Bombers were a good team and that the game would be really hard. He was afraid they would lose.
9. A person who doesn't like to pass the puck to other players.
10. Possible answer: Danny really wanted to play in the big game, but he was afraid he might not do well.

Grammar, Usage, and Mechanics ◆ *p. 60*
1. B
2. C
3. A
4. D
5. B

Unit 1 • Lesson 6
Vocabulary ◆ *p. 63*
1. B
2. A
3. B
4. C
5. A

Comprehension ◆ *pp. 64–65*
1. Part A: C   Part B: B
2. D
3. A
4. C
5. B
6. Possible answer: She had never worn a pack before. That was the best way to get her used to it.
7. 3, 1, 4, 2
8. Answers may vary.
9. Possible answer: Pam adopted and trained Ellie. She carried Ellie's pack when crossing a stream. She pushed Ellie up some ledges.
10. Possible answer: The people knew that Ellie and Pam had hiked the entire trail. They also knew how hard it must have been and that Pam and Ellie had done a great thing.

Answer Key

Unit 1 Assessment
Phonics ◆ *pp. 68–72*

1. lunch
2. then
3. wish
4. white
5. yard
6. circus
7. after
8. follow
9. garden
10. summer
11. barrel
12. drink
13. wrong
14. blink
15. trouble
16. inches
17. alive
18. hunted
19. boats
20. picking
21. third
22. paper
23. store
24. herd
25. burn

Vocabulary ◆ *pp. 73–74*

1. B
2. D
3. A
4. C
5. A
6. B
7. A
8. D
9. C
10. D

Comprehension: Cold Read ◆ *pp. 75–76*

Lexile Measure 440L
Mean Sentence Length 8.42
Mean Log Word
Frequency 3.81
Word Count 497

Comprehension ◆ *p. 77*

1. C
2. A
3. A
4. B
5. C

Grammar, Usage, and Mechanics ◆ *pp. 78–79*

1. B
2. C
3. B
4. C
5. A
6. B
7. C
8. C
9. Thanksgiving; November
10. I; Texas

Spelling ◆ *pp. 80–81*

1. C
2. D
3. A
4. C
5. B
6. B
7. A
8. D
9. C
10. B

Unit 2 • Lesson 1
Phonics ◆ *pp. 85–86*

1. cave
2. gate
3. April
4. game
5. able
6. rice
7. thrive
8. side
9. kind
10. light

Vocabulary ◆ *p. 87*

1. B
2. A
3. D
4. C
5. C

Comprehension ◆ *pp. 88–89*

1. Part A: C Part B: C
2. A
3. D
4. C
5. B
6. Possible answer: The stick seemed to calm him down. He was less angry. The stick felt comfortable and made him more creative.
7. Possible answer: He didn't know what to do. He was confused. He just stood there.
8. Possible answer: She probably had been watching him. She saw what he was doing and thought it looked interesting. She wanted to help.
9. Possible answer: He was lonely and bored because he had no friends and nothing to do.
10. Possible answer: An area outside a city but not in the woods. Maybe the house was just built because there were lots of things like wood around to build with.

Grammar, Usage, and Mechanics ◆ *p. 90*

1. flow from the Rocky Mountains.
2. stopped to watch the bears.
3. opened his eyes.

Answer Key

4. Possible answer: I like going to the library.
5. Possible answer: Where are we going after school?

Unit 2 • Lesson 2
Phonics ◆ *pp. 93–94*

1. bone
2. hope
3. most
4. joke
5. cold
6. bugle
7. huge
8. mule
9. union
10. usual

Vocabulary ◆ *p. 95*

1. D
2. B
3. B
4. A
5. A

Comprehension ◆ *pp. 96–97*

1. Part A: B Part B: D
2. A
3. C
4. A
5. C
6. Possible answer: Glaciers make deep valleys near the ocean. The glacier melts. The valleys fill up with ocean water.
7. Possible answer: There are fewer glaciers today. Some melted after the last Ice Age. More melted since the early 1900s.
8. Possible answer: Rock flour is a powder made of rock. It is made when glaciers grind rocks and soil into tiny pieces.

9. Possible answer: A crevasse can be hard to see. If you are climbing in the mountains or on a glacier, you might fall into a crevasse.
10. Possible answer: Snow falls into a place. It piles up, and the weight of the snow on top turns the bottom layers into ice.

Grammar, Usage, and Mechanics ◆ *p. 98*

1. B
2. D
3. A
4. C
5. B

Unit 2 • Lesson 3
Phonics ◆ *pp. 101–103*

1. basic
2. items
3. useful
4. music
5. post
6. longest
7. nearer
8. bigger
9. kindest
10. louder
11. knob
12. wrist
13. knot
14. wrap
15. sign

Vocabulary ◆ *p. 104*

1. C
2. A
3. D
4. C
5. A

Comprehension ◆ *pp. 105–106*

1. Part A: C Part B: B
2. B
3. A
4. D
5. A
6. Possible answer: Namazu tries to escape. He wiggles wildly. This causes earthquakes.
7. Possible answer: People live on top of his head. When his neck is sore, he stretches. This causes his head to move and the land trembles.
8. Possible answer: On the bottom is a cobra. A turtle stands on the cobra. Four elephants stand on the turtle.
9. Possible answers: He piled straw on the turtles and added soil. He made mountains and forests out of clouds.
10. Possible answer: People used things that were familiar to them. Animals are part of nature. So are earthquakes.

Grammar, Usage, and Mechanics ◆ *p. 107*

1. B
2. C
3. A
4. C
5. C

Unit 2 • Lesson 4
Phonics ◆ *pp. 110–111*

1. e_e
2. e
3. e_e
4. e

Answer Key

5. e
6. fable
7. kind
8. nose
9. eve
10. usual

Vocabulary ◆ *p. 112*
1. C
2. C
3. B
4. D
5. A

Comprehension ◆
pp. 113–114
1. Part A: A Part B: B
2. A
3. D
4. B
5. C
6. Possible answer: The plates move and grow. They rub against one another. Energy is released along faults causing earthquakes.
7. Possible answer: Both are caused by earth's plates. When energy is released on land, a seismic wave shakes the ground. When it happens under the water, a tsunami is created.
8. Possible answer: The plates interact in three ways. They can move away from each other, toward each other, and slide past each other.
9. Possible answer: Boundaries are the places where plates meet. These form cracks in Earth's crust called faults.

10. Possible answer: When earthquakes happen, newer buildings sway. This means they move back and forth. They don't fall down like older buildings.

Grammar, Usage, and Mechanics ◆ *p. 115*
1. D
2. B
3. A
4. C
5. C

Unit 2 • Lesson 5
Phonics ◆ *pp. 118–119*
1. equal
2. knee
3. east
4. read
5. deep
6. show
7. glove
8. there
9. board
10. knows

Vocabulary ◆ *p. 120*
1. C
2. D
3. B
4. A
5. C

Comprehension ◆
pp. 121–122
1. Part A: D Part B: A
2. C
3. B
4. A
5. C

6. Possible answer: The backyard was a beach. The only living things were algae. There was a volcano nearby.
7. Possible answer: They were cave people. They wore animal skins and lived in a rocky shelter. They made tools of stone.
8. Possible answer: These were Native Americans. They were cooking meat and having a harvest celebration.
9. Possible answer: A sawmill is a place where logs were cut. It had a big saw blade. It was probably powered by the water from the brook.
10. Possible answer: The story is happening in the morning. The author is just waking up. Mother said that breakfast was ready.

Grammar, Usage, and Mechanics ◆ *p. 123*
1. B
2. A
3. C
4. B
5. C

Unit 2 • Lesson 6
Vocabulary ◆ *p. 126*
1. D
2. B
3. A
4. A
5. C

Answer Key

Comprehension ◆
pp. 127–128

1. Part A: C Part B: D
2. A
3. B
4. C
5. A
6. Possible answer: Both are melted rock. Magma is found under Earth's surface. Lava is magma that comes to the surface.
7. Possible answer: The ground swells a little bit each year. This forms a bulge that might become a volcano.
8. Possible answer: The lava makes the ocean steam because it is hot. The water cools the lava. The lava hardens and forms new land.
9. Possible answer: People have tried to stop creative eruptions. They were not successful because even gentle lava flows are hard to stop.
10. Possible answer: Yes. People like to see these eruptions. Because the lava flows slowly, it isn't too dangerous. You can run away from the lava flow.

Unit 2 Assessment
Phonics ◆ *pp. 131–134*

1. b. wild
2. a. April
3. b. bite
4. a. rate
5. b. dime
6. a. no
7. b. role

8. a. humor
9. c. hose
10. b. mute
11. a. free
12. c. bonus
13. b. cable
14. c. title
15. b. unite
16. b. knelt
17. c. gnat
18. a. write
19. a. knows
20. b. design

Vocabulary ◆ *pp. 135–136*

1. B
2. D
3. A
4. C
5. D
6. A
7. B
8. D
9. C
10. D

Comprehension: Cold Read ◆ *pp. 137–138*

Lexile Measure 560L
Mean Sentence Length 10.11
Mean Log Word Frequency 3.84
Word Count 535

Comprehension ◆ *p. 139*

1. B
2. C
3. B
4. A
5. B

Grammar, Usage, and Mechanics ◆ *pp. 140–141*

1. A
2. D
3. B

4. C
5. A
6. B
7. D
8. A
9. C
10. D

Spelling ◆ *pp. 142–143*

1. B
2. D
3. C
4. A
5. C
6. B
7. A
8. D
9. C
10. B

Unit 3 • Lesson 1
Phonics ◆ *pp. 147–148*

1. stay; _ay
2. paid; ai_
3. tray; _ay
4. laid; ai_
5. play; _ay
6. trace
7. flavor
8. April
9. late
10. bale

Vocabulary ◆ *p. 149*

1. D
2. C
3. A
4. B
5. D

Comprehension ◆
pp. 150–151

1. Part A: C Part B: D
2. A
3. C
4. B
5. C

Answer Key

6. Answers may vary.

7. Possible answer: A snake is a plumber's tool. It is a long tool that is flexible. You push the snake into a clogged pipe to clean it out.

8. Possible answer: If the pest control specialist uses poison, the people have to leave the house. They can only return when the house is safe.

9. Possible answer: The garbage is covered with soil so it does not blow away. It also protects nearby water or land.

10. Possible answer: The names are in bold print so that readers can see them clearly. This helps readers remember the names of the workers.

Grammar, Usage, and Mechanics ◆ p. 152

1. C
2. A
3. D
4. B
5. D

Unit 3 • Lesson 2
Phonics ◆ pp. 155–156

1. field
2. chief
3. baby
4. penny
5. donkey
6. queen
7. underneath
8. tweet
9. helium
10. even

Vocabulary ◆ p. 157

1. D
2. A
3. C
4. B
5. C

Comprehension ◆ pp. 158–159

1. Part A: D Part B: A
2. C
3. B
4. A
5. D
6. Family, child; School, classmate; Community, neighbor
7. Possible answer: A sibling is a brother or sister. Some children have siblings. Others do not. They are a son or daughter to their parents, but they are not siblings.
8. Possible answer: Some family responsibilities are helping to make dinner, walking the dog, taking out the garbage, making your bed, setting the table.
9. Possible answer: You can listen to others, ask questions, and be courteous. You might help others or ask for help yourself.
10. Possible answer: People in a neighborhood move away. Other people move in. You might move to a new neighborhood.

Grammar, Usage, and Mechanics ◆ p. 160

1. B
2. D

3. A
4. C
5. B

Unit 3 • Lesson 3
Phonics ◆ pp. 163–165

1. sail
2. May
3. paid
4. save
5. maple
6. thumb
7. phone
8. graph
9. climb
10. numb
11. l
12. w
13. u
14. t
15. n

Vocabulary ◆ p. 166

1. A
2. C
3. B
4. C
5. B

Comprehension ◆ pp. 167–168

1. Part A: C Part B: A
2. D
3. B
4. C
5. D
6. Possible answer: The construction is taking place in a field near the author's house. The author is writing from his bedroom.
7. bulldozer, scrape up dirt; dump truck, move dirt away from field; excavator, scoop dirt out of ground; crane, lift solar panels to roof

Answer Key

8. Possible answer: The town has grown quickly. The old school is crowded. The town held a vote and decided to build a new school.

9. Possible answer: The cranes look like giant hands reaching down to pick up sticks.

10. Possible answer: The writer was interviewed by a reporter. He saw the whole construction process from his house. The interview was the coolest part of the experience.

Grammar, Usage, and Mechanics ◆ p. 169

1. C
2. A
3. D
4. B
5. B

Unit 3 • Lesson 4
Phonics ◆ pp. 172–173

1. circle
2. celery
3. icy
4. face
5. spicy
6. stage
7. huge
8. giraffe
9. age
10. ginger

Vocabulary ◆ p. 174

1. B
2. C
3. A
4. D
5. B

Comprehension ◆
pp. 175–176

1. Part A: A Part B: D
2. C
3. B
4. B
5. A
6. Jasmine Thompson, likes the new classrooms; Terrell Burton, community garden out back; Sarah Gonzalez, solar panels; Mayor Lopez, property values will go up
7. Answers may vary.
8. Possible answer: They were local and some had children who would go to the school. They did a great job and finished on time.
9. Possible answer: An inviting neighborhood seems nice. People will want to live in the neighborhood.
10. Possible answer: They counted down from ten. They cheered when the sheet fell to the ground.

Grammar, Usage, and Mechanics ◆ p. 177

1. tomatoes, onions,
2. volunteers: Andy, Rose,
3. squirrels, rabbits,
4. following: a hat, sunscreen,
5. Snow, ice,

Unit 3 • Lesson 5
Phonics ◆ pp. 180–181

1. lie
2. high
3. fly
4. pie
5. style
6. kind; i

7. mile or lime; i_e
8. child; i
9. nine; i_e
10. find; i

Vocabulary ◆ p. 182

1. B
2. A
3. D
4. A
5. C

Comprehension ◆
pp. 183–184

1. Part A: C; Part B: B
2. B
3. D
4. C
5. D
6. a. plaza; b. stone; a. seasoning
7. Possible answer: Few people came to the village. It was dark and dry. Vegetables had wilted.
8. Possible answer: They used the visitor's stone to make soup every week. They all brought something.
9. Possible answer: No, she knew it was just a stone. But it helped the village come together.
10. Possible answer: Life had been very hard. They were hungry and worried about the winter.

Grammar, Usage, and Mechanics ◆ p. 185

1. C
2. B
3. D
4. A
5. C

Answer Key

Unit 3 • Lesson 6
Vocabulary ◆ p. 188

1. B
2. D
3. C
4. A
5. C

Comprehension ◆ pp. 189–190

1. Part A: C   Part B: D
2. A
3. B
4. D
5. A
6. Street Sweeper, swishes along; Window Dresser, a mannequin dressed; Late-Night Radio DJ, they choose the songs; Security guard, this job is about protecting
7. Possible answer: It tricks them into sleeping at night. Then the stay awake during the day for visitors.
8. Possible answer: The workers meet at the all-night cafe. They probably talk about their work.
9. Possible answer: The road worker makes it hard for the truck driver. The road work slows down the traffic, including the truck driver.
10. Possible answer: The hawk's nest is mentioned in the part about bridge painters. It shows that the workers care about the hawks and paint around the nest.

Unit 3 Assessment
Phonics ◆ pp. 193–197

1. a. wait
2. b. sway
3. c. state
4. a. apron
5. c. frame
6. a. tally
7. b. money
8. c. beam
9. c. thief
10. b. monkey
11. comb
12. photo
13. calf
14. wrist
15. plumber
16. b. pace
17. a. pencils
18. a. city
19. c. fancy
20. a. frigid
21. b. tight
22. c. tiger
23. c. fried
24. a. cry
25. b. bright

Vocabulary ◆ pp. 198–199

1. B
2. C
3. A
4. D
5. C
6. B
7. C
8. D
9. A
10. C

Comprehension: Cold Read ◆ pp. 200–201

Lexile Measure 570L
Mean Sentence Length 9.96
Mean Log Word Frequency 3.79
Word Count 478

Comprehension ◆ p. 202

1. Part A: C   Part B: B
2. D
3. A
4. C
5. B

Grammar, Usage, and Mechanics ◆ pp. 203–204

1. C
2. B
3. D
4. Stores, hotels, and restaurants lined the streets.
5. The events are as follows: softball, awards, and picnic.
6. B
7. A
8. D
9. C
10. C

Spelling ◆ pp. 205–206

1. A
2. D
3. C
4. A
5. D
6. B
7. A
8. C
9. D
10. A